GROWING UP GREEK IN CHICAGO

The Ups and Downs of an Ethnic Identity

ALEXANDER RASSOGIANIS

outskirts
press

GROWING UP GREEK IN CHICAGO
The Ups and Down of an Ethnic Identity
All Rights Reserved.
Copyright © 2023 Alexander Rassogianis
v4.0

The opinions expressed in this manuscript are solely the opinions of the author and do not represent the opinions or thoughts of the publisher. The author has represented and warranted full ownership and/or legal right to publish all the materials in this book.

This book may not be reproduced, transmitted, or stored in whole or in part by any means, including graphic, electronic, or mechanical without the express written consent of the publisher except in the case of brief quotations embodied in critical articles and reviews.

Outskirts Press, Inc.
http://www.outskirtspress.com

Paperback ISBN: 978-1-9772-5972-1
Hardback ISBN: 978-1-9772-6073-4

Cover Photo © 2023 Alexander Rassogianis. All rights reserved - used with permission.

Outskirts Press and the "OP" logo are trademarks belonging to Outskirts Press, Inc.

PRINTED IN THE UNITED STATES OF AMERICA

For my brother John and my sister Pauline.

The foundation they laid enabled me to use their examples as guidance for the direction my life would take.

From
Alexander
to Athena.
Best wishes,

2023

Cover photo: left to right, my brother, John, my mother, Anna, my sister, Pauline and my father, Constantine, 1945.

Life is about accepting the challenges along the way, choosing to keep moving forward, and savoring the journey.

                                        Roy T. Bennett, *The Light in the Heart*

Life is not a problem to be solved, but a reality to be experienced.

                                                  Soren Kierkegaard

Life is sometimes made up of fleeting moments. Cherish them for they will be gone in an instant.

                                                              Author

CONTENTS

What's in a Name?	1
Searching	3
The Suburban Trek	6
A Very Good Kid	10
The Heart Is the Center	12
A High-Profile Murder	17
Good Morning, Mr. Darrow	20
A Renaissance Man	24
A Brutal War	28
Period Of Adjustment	30
Do Unto Others	34
Convalescence	37
Camaraderie	40
The Jail and the Warden	71
The Michigan Wonderland	79
Home Sweet Home	83
Camp George	89
Badge of Honor	94
Obey the Scout Motto	99
Working on Up	106
Step Up to the Plate	111
Sibling Rivalry	113
You Need to Be Involved	119
The Grecian Melodies Hour Is on the Air	122
Is She a Greek Girl?	125

Greek Here and There	131
In Retrospect	136
About the Author	139

WHAT'S IN A NAME?

I never fully realized, or even understood, what the influence of growing up in a Greek environment would have on me until I was much older. Up until then, it was a tag line I was stuck with, whether I liked it or not. It wasn't that I was against being the son of Greek immigrants or anything like that. I just wanted to be like everyone else. I wanted to fit in, especially when I was in elementary school. I wanted to be *American*. Who at that age didn't want to be accepted? Those were the worst years for me. All of my friends at school had what I thought were normal names, such as Bill, Joe, Bobby, Frank, and Tom. Even the names of my schools—General George Armstrong Custer, and President Abraham Lincoln—were as American as you could get.

Here I was with the name Alexander Constantine Rassogianis. I ask you how I could possibly fit in with a name like that? It wasn't possible to hide it, and I couldn't exactly run away. I was looking for a way of getting around it. The answer was improvisation. Since nobody knew that Constantine was my middle name, I thought I would keep it quiet. Who used middle names anyway? I didn't tell anyone and nobody asked. That settled that!

I hated the name Alexander when I was growing up, and it would upset me from time to time that my parents selected it. I was named after an uncle who died when I was about eight years old. When I told my father of my feelings, he told me that it was a great name, and that one day I would think differently about it. He said the day would come when I would thank him. I didn't believe it.

My immediate problem was what to do with it. Alexander became Alex, and Alex became Al. That was it. That became the answer to my problem. I was Al. It was as American as apple pie. It fit in, and was as normal in my world as my favorite lunchtime programs of *Uncle Johnny Coons* and *Two-Ton Baker*.

Everyone started calling me Al. I was Al on the playground and in my neighborhood on Saturdays, but inside the classroom was another matter. My teachers never referred to me as Al. It was either Alexander or Alex. I cringed every time I heard these names. My seventh-grade English teacher at Lincoln Junior High School, Mrs. Hartsough, put a little twist on the name. She called me Alec. That brought a few snickers from some of my classmates. I suppose she was thinking of some character out of nineteenth-century English literature, or perhaps Alec Guinness was a favorite actor of hers. I don't really know. I had to put up with her five days a week, and I felt somewhat uncomfortable going to her class because of it. The only other exception was my father, who always referred to me as Ali. I started to appreciate my name later and realized how foolish my outlook was, but it took a while.

SEARCHING

I was in my late twenties when I got the nostalgia bug to search for my roots. The first thing to do was to start with my birth. My brother John, my sister Pauline, and I were born at Woodlawn Hospital on the South Side of Chicago—just south of the University of Chicago campus. It was located on the corner of 60th Street and Drexel Avenue. My mother's physician, Dr. Sotirakos (Soter), was affiliated with Woodlawn and even lived nearby. He was born in Greece, but became a genuine "South Sider" for the rest of his life.

By the time it took me to become interested in seeing the building where we were born at 6060 S. Drexel Avenue, it was completely gone. I had to settle for staring at an empty lot mixed with dirt, grass, a few scattered weeds, and some rocks. It must have been a small hospital because the size of the lot was nothing you would expect for a hospital.

I parked the car across the street and crossed over to the deserted corner. I just stood there and stared at the empty space. A few university students passed me on the sidewalk, totally oblivious as to what I was doing there. I guess their minds were preoccupied with their own problems. Within two or three minutes I formed a picture in my mind as to how the hospital may have looked. I may be overexaggerating, but I honestly thought of that corner as a shrine. I imagined people walking in and out, including my mother and father.

There they were—in broad daylight with worried looks on their faces in anticipation of what was to occur. I visualized my father parking his car, which was probably a Buick or a Mercury, and escorting my mother to the emergency room. This was repeated two more times, for there were three of us born there. As I thought of them, a warm glow embraced my body. I was overcome with emotion, and it remained with me for at least thirty minutes or so before I left. I told myself that I would return someday, but I never did.

My grandfather, John, and my uncle Alex opened the St. Louis Ice Cream Parlor on St. Louis Avenue and 26th Street, also on the South Side—most likely in 1912 or 1913. My uncle George joined them in 1914. My father graduated from the Lykios (Lyceum) high school in Sparta and passed all the exams for the University of Athens. Unfortunately, he didn't get very far. He was drafted and served in the Greek army for five years during the Balkan Wars with Bulgaria and was almost killed twice. At the end of the fifth year, he suffered the first of many nervous breakdowns. He arrived in Chicago in 1924, and joined his father and brothers at the candy store.

The store was situated in the neighborhood known as Pilsen, which was predominantly Czech and Slovak at the time. It was well-known in that area for having quality products and welcoming customers with a grand sense of hospitality. There was even an article in the *Denni Hlasetel*, the local Czech newspaper, about Uncle Alex. The caption read: "Did you know that Alex the Greek, owner of the ice cream parlor on 26th Street, speaks fluent Czech?" I'm sure he learned a lot from his patrons, but I'm sure his girlfriends in the area contributed to his weekly education in linguistics.

I drove down 26th Street in the spring of 2015 on my way to jury duty at Cook County Criminal Court on 26th Street and California Avenue. I slowed down when I reached the corner where the store was, but the building was completely gone. In fact, the entire corner was torn down and reduced to rubble. I was looking at another prairie similar to the one where the hospital used to be. What a sad sight it was. It meant that the two earliest structures associated with our family in Chicago were nonexistent.

My father told me that the entire entrance to the ice-cream parlor, including the front door and two windows, was relocated to a laundromat several blocks south and west of the building. This was done sometime in the 1970s. I never tried to locate it.

I know the family used to live on St. Louis Avenue in the first apartment building south of the alley, and I've often thought of knocking on the front door someday and asking the current resident if I could take a look inside. If I did and told whoever answered the door that I was searching for my roots, he probably would think I was crazy or perhaps would slam the door in my face. I doubt if I would have ever succeeded, but I never made the effort to do it.

THE SUBURBAN TREK

The business was moved to the corner of Roosevelt Road and Grove Avenue in Berwyn in the early 1930s and called Alex's Sweet Shop. I don't know the reason why they moved, but it was obviously a better location. My father and Uncle Alex had a building constructed that resembled a castle. The architect of this mini-chateau was a friend of my father's named Evgenni (Eugene), who I believe was also from Sparta. The building included a spacious backyard, and the three or four maple trees were enough to provide shade from the sun on hot summer days. One of my favorite photos is of my parents facing each other near some ornamental bushes, with my mother holding a white dog they had as a pet in the late 1930s.

I was only eight years old when they closed the store, but the images I have are as vivid as ever. It was well decorated and colorful, especially at Christmas and Easter, when they offered ornamental baskets of assorted candies. It was an exciting place. There were wooden booths by the west windows and large tables in the middle.

One of the ceiling fans was attached to a model airplane and was tucked away in the southeast corner. There was a back room where both my uncles Alex and George lived. The accommodations were definitely spartan—two beds, a bathroom, and a small table. Decorations were nonexistent. It was as dreary as could be, but I guess it served its purpose.

I used to run around the tables with a long string in my hand so our cat, named Sugar, would chase me. She never gave up on the chase, and I was always exhausted right before I stopped. I had so much fun. My honorary job was to empty the cigarette cartons and stack the cigarettes in a rack on the wall. I took it seriously and learned every brand name by heart. My favorite was Philip Morris. A poster of Little Johnny, the hotel bellboy, was prominently situated in the front of the store with the words "Call for Philip Morris" across the top. I was always excited when I heard his call on the radio and later, on television. I just thought he was a neat guy.

My second favorite was Pall Mall, due to its dark red label and its catchy phrase—"Outstanding and—they are mild." Uncle Alex smoked Pall Mall, but my father and Uncle George did not smoke at all. My father picked up the habit later in his life, and it included smoking dreadful-smelling cigars. Another brand I distinctly remember was Herbert Tareyton.

Apparently, placing cigarettes in their proper place was the only chore I was able to perform. We had a popcorn machine located near the entrance, but I never tried to learn how to operate it, or perhaps I wasn't trusted enough to do so. What can you expect from a nine-year-old?

I don't believe my brother, sister, and I fully realized how hard my father and uncles worked to make their business successful. Life was easier for us because of their years of sacrifice. Like thousands of other Greek immigrants, they were willing to do whatever was necessary to succeed. This meant hard work and very long hours. Sometimes the income was good and sometimes it wasn't. It took perseverance and, I'm sure, a burning desire to succeed. They were guaranteed absolutely nothing.

The confectionary business of the Greeks in the United States grew at a phenomenal rate throughout the country, especially between 1895 and 1915. By 1925, thousands of ice-cream parlors and candy shops were in existence in most of the large metropolitan areas of the country. New York City had a large number of shops, since it was one of the main centers of the Greek population, but none of these could compare with Chicago. According to one estimate, there were approximately 925 confectionaries in the city as early as 1906.

The local newspaper *Hellinikos Astir* labeled the city as the "Mecca of the Candy Business," noting that "practically every busy corner in Chicago is occupied by a Greek candy store." It also asserted that 70 percent of the Greek candy merchants who were doing business in other cities once lived in Chicago and received their training there as well.

It is rather difficult to imagine what it was like to work between fourteen and fifteen hours a day, seven days a week, and not really know whether you were going to keep your business. To go out of business was to begin a period of despair. There was no alternative but to keep going. It was often stated among Greek immigrants that shop owners worked so many hours that they were basically "married" to the business. My uncle Alex and my uncle George decided that it was impractical to live anywhere else but in the back room of the store.

I recall my father telling me that the landlord of the building on 26th Street would knock on the front door of the store at 6 a.m. on the first day of every month to collect the rent. Most of the time, they would remain open longer than usual just to earn enough to avoid eviction. At the Berwyn location, they would open the door at 11 a.m. and close at 11 p.m.

Prior to opening for business, they would all be in the basement starting at 6 a.m., making chocolates. This went on seven days a week. They employed several women from the neighborhood to help in this effort, and I remember them as being very cordial ladies. They would always smile at me whenever I came downstairs. I recall asking my uncle George about those years:

"During the early days there was no money. We would barely make enough to get by. I worked all day long. I couldn't count the hours. I worked probably eighteen hours a day. We sold a lot of sodas for five cents, but barely made enough money to pay the rent. We would kill ourselves just to make a nickel. I never had a happy day in America. It was only work."

A VERY GOOD KID

My uncle Alex hired a high school boy named Bob Jacklin, who lived on the same block as the store, to make local deliveries and do a few odd jobs. About four years ago I needed to rent some tools for a project we were working on at a building I own on Cermak Road. I went to Jack's Tool Rental on 26th Street in Berwyn to see if they had what I needed. An older man, perhaps in his eighties, helped me find everything I was looking for. He was very polite and had a pleasant demeanor about him. We walked back to the cash register at the counter, and I made out a check to Jack's Tool Rental.

He looked at the check and obviously noticed my name. He looked directly at me and, with an extra-wide grin on his face, said, "Gus, George, and Alex."

Completely dumbfounded, I replied: "Yes, they were my two uncles and my father. How did you know that?"

"I used to work for them when I was in high school. My name is Bob Jacklin."

"It's a pleasure to meet you, Bob."

"You must be Gus's son?"

"Yes, that's right. What do you remember about those days, Bob?"

"They were nice guys. They always treated me well. I'll tell you one thing, though."

"I know what you're going to say," I said. "You got tired

of my uncle Alex's jokes?"

"Oh no. Not at all. He entertained everybody. What I wanted to say is that they all worked extremely hard. They didn't have much of a life. I respected what they achieved. Believe me."

"Of course, you know about the robbery while Alex was there at night?"

"Yes. They hit him pretty bad. They took me to see him, but he couldn't recognize me. He had no idea who I was."

I reminisced with him for about twenty minutes or so before he had to go back to work.

"Bob, I have a photo of the three of them in the middle of the store surrounded by Easter baskets. I will make a copy for you."

"I'd love to have it," he said as he waved goodbye.

THE HEART IS THE CENTER

My uncle Alex had quite a personality. Some people used to come to our ice-cream parlor just to see him and talk to him. You might say he was the drawing attraction. He called all of the little boys "peewee." I can still remember the dialogue as though I heard it yesterday.

"Hi, peewee."

"Hi," the little boy would respond.

"How are you doing today?"

Sometimes the mother would have to prod her shy little son to answer.

"I'm okay."

"Say, peewee, I'll bet I know where you live!"

"No, you don't." The answer was always the same.

"Oh yes I do," Uncle Alex said assuredly.

The little youngster was certain that my uncle did not know where he lived. How could he? My uncle never saw him come out of his home. I'm sure the boy thought it was impossible.

Once again, the boy responded, "No, you don't."

Uncle Alex looked at him with a wide grin on his face and then chuckled with a big surprise.

"You live in a house, don't you? You don't live in a barn?"

Everyone would laugh, including my uncle. This continued hundreds of times, and nobody got tired of it. Every time he finished having fun, he would stuff a bag of buttered popcorn in the little boy's front pocket and make him smile. He was a generous guy.

He was a very strong and well-built man in his younger years. He was more muscular than most men, and he often challenged others to arm-wrestling duels. One of my favorite stories is one my father told me many times. The chief of police in Berwyn visited our candy store often and was a good friend of my father and my uncles. He was a big, burly man of German stock, and he stood at about six feet, three inches. He had an imposing stature for sure. He arm-wrestled Uncle Alex several times and lost each time. He was getting frustrated that the Greek always beat him.

My father always gave a detailed description of how the chief was dressed. I guess he saw some humor in it. He had a double-breasted blue uniform, a large, shiny star pinned to his chest, an oversized club dangling from his belt, and a handsome mustache. He almost looked like a creation of Mack Sennett rather than the city police chief.

Anyway, he came into the store one day, and Uncle Alex challenged him once again, but not to arm-wrestling. My uncle had a brand-new opportunity for his friend to finally achieve an overdue victory. This was his big chance—a shining moment!

"I'll make a bet with you."

"What's the bet?" asked the chief.

"You're not going to like it," warned Uncle Alex.

"Go ahead. What is it?" The officer was very curious.

"I'll bet you that if we shake hands and hold our grip on each other, I'll force you all the way down to the floor."

It was a version of arm-wrestling, but a little different. The police chief stared at him with amazement and disbelief. He looked at my father and Uncle George as though telling them that their brother was absolutely insane.

"Get out of here. You're not serious, are you?"

"Yes, I am," my uncle said with an air of confidence.

"You don't know what you're talking about," he shot back.

"Oh, yes, I do."

Uncle Alex was really putting him on the spot. Here he was, the chief of police—and a big, brawny one to boot—in front of my uncles, my father, and several customers who forgot about their hot fudge sundaes and their banana splits for a while and wanted to see some action instead. He had no choice but to concede to the challenge.

"All right," he admitted. "I can't wait to see this."

My uncle wanted to clarify one stipulation before they shook hands. "Before we start," Uncle Alex said with a toned-down voice, "you've got to promise me that, if I do it, you won't hold it against me."

"Oh, no, you don't have to worry about that," he conceded.

"Your friendship is important to all of us, and we want it to remain so."

The last thing all of them wanted was for the police chief to be angry at them. They certainly needed the protection of the police department to operate a business.

"We'll always be friends," the chief guaranteed him.

"Besides, you're not going to do what you said anyway, so what's the difference?"

They shook hands. Their grip on each other was as firm as could be. Just then, another customer walked in and couldn't believe what he was witnessing. He stood at the front door and didn't move an inch. His mouth was wide open, and he almost forgot what he had come in for. It was becoming more intense by the minute. The chief started to bend. He was falling lower and lower.

His face was turning red and showing a great sense of anguish. He was struggling to maintain his stance. You could see the contraction of the lines on his face and the squinting of his grayish eyes. He tried desperately to stand erect at all costs. Within about twenty seconds, his oversized frame flopped down on the hardwood floor.

"Son of a bitch," he yelled out, looking straight up at my uncle. "How the hell did you do that?"

"I told you I could."

All the brothers showed a little good faith by helping him off the floor. When he got up, they straightened out his uniform and dusted him off a bit. He looked at my uncle and began to laugh.

"Son of a bitch," he said one more time. I guess there wasn't much else to say. He continued to laugh as loud as he could.

I didn't know my uncle Alex very well. After all, I was only a second grader at George Armstrong Custer Elementary School on the corner of Oak Park Avenue and 14th Street in Berwyn when he died. I remember fractured thoughts of times we spent together and some of the things he told me. One of those times, he took me by the hand to a small diner on Roosevelt Road several doors from our candy store for pie a la mode. It was a wonderful treat for me, especially the ice cream.

He would tell me stories about Alexander the Great on the front porch of the apartment we lived in down the alley from our store. My uncle George and my father were both present, and they were getting a kick out of me and the things I said.

"How big was Alexander the Great, Ali?" my uncle asked with a smile.

My uncles, my father, and my mother called me Ali. To my brother and sister, I was always Al.

"He was big," I answered, thinking this was what they wanted to hear.

"How big was he?"

"Real big," I said with strong determination in my voice. They all laughed. "Was he as big as the tree outside?" I wasn't trying to be funny with my question.

"Oh, much bigger than that, Ali."

"Was he bigger than the building across the street?"

"Oh yes," all three declared in one synchronized voice.

The question-and-answer session continued for quite a while until they finally explained what they were driving at. I certainly enjoyed the attention afforded me.

A HIGH-PROFILE MURDER

One of the most intriguing subjects concerning my uncle Alex was the execution of a murderer. I recall him telling me he attended the actual hanging of a man named Wanderer. I doubted this story for many years because I never thought anyone could have a name like that. I thought my uncle misheard the facts of the case or perhaps didn't know what he was talking about.

While doing research for my history classes in college, I came across the case of an army veteran in Chicago who murdered his pregnant wife and another man in the vestibule of an apartment building at 4732 North Campbell Avenue. The murders took place on June 21, 1920. The former soldier served in France during World War I and became a second lieutenant before being discharged. His name was Carl Wanderer. I realized I hadn't given my uncle the credit he deserved. He knew exactly what he was talking about after all.

Before and after his army service, Carl Wanderer worked in his father's butcher shop at 2711 North Western Avenue. He married a girl he had known since their grammar school days named Ruth Johnson, who was the daughter of Swedish immigrants. Carl and Ruth lived with her parents at the Campbell Avenue address, but Ruth continually pressed her husband of the need to have a home of their own, especially with a child on the way.

Carl grew irritated that Ruth was expecting a baby. He felt his life had become too restricted, and it was said he wanted to go back in the Army. He was also attracted to a young girl who frequented the Wanderer butcher shop, named Julia Schmitt. He began seeing her regularly and told his wife that he was socializing with old army buddies every time he left the house. Still, the art of deception wasn't good enough for him.

Growing more frustrated by the day, he concocted a plan that led to the murder of his wife and her unborn child. He recruited the services of a drifter who lived on Madison Street and told him he would pay him ten dollars if he staged a robbery of Wanderer and his wife. He told the man, who would become known as the "ragged stranger," that he wanted to impress his wife by defending her from a thief. Of course, it was lie.

Wanderer told the drifter that he and his wife would go to a movie at the Pershing Theatre in Lincoln Square that evening and then walk home. The drifter followed them all the way back and into the vestibule of Ruth's parents' apartment, where they were held up at gunpoint. Rather than beat up the drifter and take his gun away, Wanderer shot him, turned the gun on his wife, and fired several times.

He told the police the drifter killed his wife and then he shot the drifter. Later at the trial, the truth was revealed, partially due to the investigative reporting of Ben Hecht of the *Chicago Daily News* and Charles MacArthur of the *Chicago Examiner*. Wanderer had supplied the pistol that the drifter used. He received the death penalty and was hanged at the Cook County Jail at 54 West Hubbard Street on September 30, 1921.

I often questioned why my uncle was present at the execution. I can't blame him for his curiosity since the case merited national headlines. Hundreds of people gathered outside the courthouse every day of the trial. I believe he had to receive an invitation to attend; otherwise, the jail grounds to the north of the court where the gallows were located would be overwhelmed by the public.

The question is who invited him? He was well-liked at the St. Louis Ice Cream Parlor on 26th Street and St. Louis Avenue, and the article about him in the Czech newspaper *Denni Hlasatel* helped spread his popularity in the area.

Perhaps one of his customers had some political connections, or perhaps one of his "brothers" at the Masonic lodge pulled some strings for him to attend. I wish I had asked more questions long ago, but then again I was only eight years old when he died. Nevertheless, I am still perplexed as to how he was present at the execution of one of the most notorious criminals in Chicago history.

GOOD MORNING, MR. DARROW

Another perplexing episode concerning my uncle involved the invention of a refrigeration system. Uncle Alex, together with another man, created a device for freezing and hardening food stuffs. Their focus was on the freezing of ice cream, which made sense since both were involved in the ice-cream business.

My father always told me, especially in later years, that they were cheated by the lawyers who were involved in the patent process. I remember he was very bitter regarding lawyers because of this, and I recall the dialogue between us quite clearly:

"Ali, please don't disgrace our family name."

"Why would I do that, and how could I do that."

"By becoming a lawyer," he said bluntly.

"What do you mean?" I was puzzled.

"They are lice who will suck your blood for money," he told me in an emotional voice. "Please don't disgrace my name by becoming one."

"Certainly, they aren't all that way, are they?"

He didn't answer.

I still don't know, to this day, how they were supposedly cheated by their lawyers with regard to the handling of the patent process. Was this possible? They applied for the patent in 1928, and it was awarded in 1930. Were they misled somehow after the patent process was concluded? I am not aware of the means by which this could occur.

However, it was serious enough to merit an appointment with attorney Clarence Darrow, who gained national recognition in 1924 by defending Nathan Leopold and Richard Loeb for the thrill killing of fourteen-year-old Bobby Franks in Chicago's Kenwood neighborhood.

I don't know if Darrow gave them any fruitful advice that would benefit them. I don't believe he did. My father told me that the famed attorney looked at them and said, "You poor Greeks. After all these years you are still in bondage." I interpret this, in part, to saying that something happened that affected them in a harmful or disturbing manner. People "in bondage" are obviously victims of those who yield more influence and power.

Things didn't get any better for Uncle Alex. He was hit over the head with a blunt instrument at the ice-cream parlor on Roosevelt Road during a robbery in 1942. The blow was so severe that he never fully recovered. Two men came in shortly before closing time, late in the evening. He served them and returned to the last booth in the store, where he had been reading the evening newspaper. Unfortunately, he was facing the rear wall and could not see what they were doing.

It was easy for them to strike the blow. He was rushed to MacNeal Hospital, and when my mother, father, and Uncle George arrived, he could not recognize them. He told them they looked very familiar, but he wasn't sure who they were. I remember my father telling me years later that my uncle didn't even know his own name. After a long illness and a partial recovery, he finally died in 1954.

I was only eight years old at the time, but I remember the day quite vividly. My uncle George came to my bed in the early morning. He got down on his knees. "*O theos, o Alexis epethane!*" he cried out. "Uncle Alex died."

"George, come and help me," my father pleaded with him. Unlike my uncle, my father maintained his composure throughout the morning. Uncle George didn't respond to my father's frantic plea for help. He didn't even glance up at him when he entered my bedroom. He was still on his knees weeping profusely to me.

"Uncle Alex died." He repeated it several times. Uncle Alex had been sleeping in the front porch, and my bedroom wasn't far from there. I was stunned. I hadn't experienced anyone dying before. Worse than that, I didn't know how to handle the actions of Uncle George. The poor guy was in bad shape. My father tried to console him, but he really took it hard. I believe I made an attempt to say something that would be soothing, but I wasn't successful. After all, I was just a kid.

Uncle George came to Chicago as a teenager to work with Uncle Alex at the ice-cream parlor on the South Side. We all believe that Uncle Alex, who was considerably older, took on a parental role. We think he became a father figure for his younger brother. Uncle George came to my bed to grieve because I was the one who was named after his older mentor. It was a sad situation. Years later, he would ask me the same question.

"Do you remember Uncle Alex?"

He always had a smile on his face when he looked at me and waited for my answer.

"Sure, I do. I can't forget," I would respond.

There was always a follow-up question, and it was always the same one.

"Do you know how much he loved you?"

Then he would answer the question himself.

"He loved you very much."

I never tried to say anything before he did, because I understood how much he wanted to utter those words. All he had left were memories.

A RENAISSANCE MAN

Considering the numerous hardships my father faced in his life, he still managed to be successful in almost everything he set out to do. I look at him as a Renaissance Man.

He left for Chicago in 1925 to help my uncles and my grandfather at the St. Louis Ice Cream Parlor. Later, they moved to the corner of Roosevelt Road and Grove Avenue in Berwyn. An acquaintance of his, an architect also from Sparta, designed the castle-like structure that would be the new home for their business.

Despite the periodic breakdowns, he maintained his writing skills and had his own column in the *Greek Press,* which was one of the city's Greek language newspapers. Most of his articles focused on philosophy, history, and current and cultural events. He was very good at mathematics and classical Greek.

What gave him a great sense of satisfaction was receiving phone calls from admirers from across the country who complimented him on his articles. He often spent hours talking on the phone, discussing what he wrote and answering questions, especially with his friend Dr. Koutris of Houston, Texas. He also spent many hours discussing Greek Orthodox Church affairs with Nicholas Cassavetes in New York.

My father had the intelligence, foresight, and determination to assure that his family would have a better life than he did. He made investments in real estate that enabled my brother, sister, and me to obtain college degrees. He also had a summer home built in Stevensville, Michigan, which we enjoyed all of our lives up to the present. He was a businessman and an intellectual, which is not an easy thing to accomplish.

He was also an accomplished mandolin player who delighted us from time to time, displaying his skill and talent on the popular eight-stringed instrument. On many evenings in Michigan, we would get together with our next-door neighbors, the Demeur family, and Dr. Demeur would accompany my father on the Cretan lyra. When they really got going, it was a fantastic show.

Related to his love of music was his role of a *psalti* (kanter) every Sunday in the Annunciation Greek Orthodox Church in nearby Benton Harbor. He made a great accompanist to his close friend Father Moulas. It was a joy for him to participate in the church he loved so much.

One thing I must bring out is that he was not a social climber. He never put on false airs as to who he was and where he came from. We never lived in a rich suburb; he never owned a Cadillac automobile and certainly never had his initials on his license plates. In fact, he looked down upon those who bragged about how much money they had, including other Greeks.

I recall one evening when he was on the phone for at least forty-five minutes but didn't do much talking. Apparently, the person on the other end was giving him an earful. When he finally finished, he looked at me with a disgusted expression on his face.

"Who was that?" I asked.

"It was a man from church who doesn't live far from us."

"What did you two discuss?" I was rather inquisitive.

"He spent all of that time telling me how many buildings he owns and how much money he has."

"That's why you didn't say much?"

"What could I say? I had to sit here and listen to it."

"I could tell you were rather bored."

"I was. This man has nothing else to talk about. I wish I hadn't answered the phone."

I knew that he obviously preferred discussions that were thought-provoking and interesting. He had an intellectual mind but was also diligent in matters of business. Had he remained in Greece, he would have become a priest. He told me this many times. To be blunt about it—he was a smart guy. I bought my first car when I graduated from college and began teaching in Chicago. It was a sleek, stylish royal-blue MGB sports car, complete with a stick shift on the floor.

When my father saw my new car, he asked me why I bought a sports car. I told him about the many amenities the car gave me. I told him the gas mileage was very good, and it was easy to park anywhere. He looked at me and said: "Let's face it, you bought that car for one reason, and one reason only—to impress the girls. Don't tell me about gas mileage." You couldn't put anything past him, that's for sure.

My father went back to Greece and married my mother in Goritsa, Sparta, in 1935. Both of my grandmothers grew up together in Chrisefa, Sparta, and were very close friends. It's obvious they were instrumental in arranging the match. My parents came back and lived in an apartment at 1241 Home Avenue, just about three blocks from the store. Later, my father bought a four-unit apartment building at 1230 S. Oak Park Avenue—around the corner and down the alley from the candy store.

All of us grew up at this location. I always thought my father should have bought a single-family home for us, but

I realize now that he was using common sense and logical thinking to invest in a four-unit structure so the rents from the other three could help pay the mortgage. My two uncles lived in the back of the store, and the three of them would take turns walking to our apartment, where my mother would have meals waiting for them.

I can visualize now how the immigrant families stuck together and became one family unit for the purpose of survival. My uncles were not married to my mother, and yet she cooked for them every day. There were other families who lived in the same apartment and were aunts, uncles, or cousins. They did so because they had to. These were sacrifices made by millions of immigrants. Those of us who were born here sometimes find it difficult to comprehend the sacrifices of those who came before us.

A BRUTAL WAR

I wish I could go back in time to talk to my father about his army days. Spending all those years in frontline service took its toll on him, resulting in the series of nervous breakdowns. Nobody knew about post-traumatic stress disorder in those days, but I'm sure that's what he had. I know nothing of his basic training days and very little of the battles he was in. He didn't talk much about it.

I regret not asking him about the training he received and about the men who served under him. I wonder today if he could remember their names and where they were from. I wish I knew how many of them lived through the experience. In a photo we have of my father's platoon, in the bottom right-hand corner there is a soldier who looks like a high school boy, or even younger. To this day I often wonder what his name was and where he called home. I wish I could have asked him who this boy under his command was.

There are only three things I remember him describing to me:

My father's platoon had run out of water during a heated campaign against the Bulgarians inside Serbia, which was an ally of Greece. He told me how they were literally drinking mud on the ground through handkerchiefs. The water level in a creek was so low that there was nothing to actually drink. They were lucky to settle for a little moisture in their mouths.

The second incident he told me about is that a bomb had landed exactly where he was kneeling on the ground during a battle. His men thought he was killed, but a minute before the explosive landed where he was, he had moved to another position. Had he stayed, he would have been dead for sure. His men were exuberant that he was still alive, but initially shocked to see him when he suddenly appeared.

His third vivid recollection also took place in the middle of a heated battle. In this scenario, the Bulgarians were advancing rapidly on the Greek and Serbian positions on a sloped embankment. One of the Greek machine-gunners couldn't fire because his weapon had jammed. He kept trying to adjust it, but to no avail. It was raining and there was heavy smoke and confusion everywhere.

A young lieutenant crawled over to him and yelled at him to get it going. The gunner told him he just couldn't get it together. He kept saying, "I'm trying. I'm trying." At that point the lieutenant pulled out his pistol and pointed it at the gunner's head. He yelled out to him, "Fix it now or I'll blow your brains out." In an effort that took about ten seconds, the machine gun was repaired and the gunner was firing indiscriminately against the approaching infantry.

I asked my father if the lieutenant would have killed him, and he said he had asked himself the same question several times. He honestly didn't know.

PERIOD OF ADJUSTMENT

As a teenager, my mother's father, who was a doctor in Goritsa-Sparta, sent her and her sister Thea (Aunt) Matoula to a French academy operated by the Ursuline Order on the Cycladic Greek island of Naxos. My mother spoke fluent French and learned to paint and play the piano. She once said that the four years she spent as a student on Naxos were the best years of her life. As fate would have it, she would never return.

She had a difficult time adjusting to life in America. I don't really know if she had the desire to come here or not, but once she arrived, it was not what she expected. To make matters worse, she sat at home alone every day while my father was working at the candy store. The hours were long and lonely. In the early days, as soon as he left for work in the morning, my mother's tears would start to flow. The woman who lived downstairs, Mrs. Grace Dombrow, heard the cries and reached out to her in a gracious sense of understanding and sympathy. They became close friends, spending mornings together talking and drinking Greek coffee.

The world my mother knew in Greece was gone forever. Her mother, father, three sisters, and many other relatives never left, and it would be approximately twenty years before she would see them again. Hundreds of letters would travel back and forth across the Atlantic for a long time. It was her only connection to her loved ones. There were no easy phone calls in those days and no airliner to board for a day's journey across the ocean. Millions of immigrants from many countries suffered through a long period of adjustment.

A wonderful outlet for her was the Oakwyn Theater, located directly next door to our ice-cream parlor. It was a small neighborhood venue typical of hundreds in the Chicago area in those days. It was owned by Mr. Charouhas, a friend of both my uncles and my father. Instead of waiting for my father at home or in the store until closing time at ten o'clock, my mother would walk over to the theater and watch the latest movies. The owner never allowed her to pay.

I used to stand in front of the theater and stare at the posters of coming movies. One day Mr. Charouhas stood there and stared at me without saying a word. I stared right back at him with a determined look on my face as though he wasn't going to intimidate me, but deep down inside I was afraid. I was wearing my Daniel Boone coonskin hat with the tail in the back. I was proud.

Since new double features were shown at least three times a week, my mother learned quite a bit of English in the theatre. Her favorite actors were Irene Dunne, Carole Lombard, Clark Gable, John Garfield, and Tyrone Power. Greer Garson was another actor she admired. I remember how she described John Garfield one day: "Behind that tough guy image, he was a good man with a kind heart." To this day, I don't know how she came to this conclusion.

Some immigrants learned English by attending evening classes at their local high schools. Others learned from friends and relatives or merely by general daily contact with the public. Although she took classes later at Plato School of the Assumption Church, my mother often admitted that the scores of movies she saw at the Oakwyn were invaluable in learning how to speak this strange-sounding language of her adopted homeland.

In later years, we would all pile into the car on Sunday evenings and head for the North Side to see Greek movies. The first theatre to show films from Greece was the Avon on Fullerton Avenue, followed by the Commodore on Irving Park Road. I enjoyed the films, especially the comedies. I also, in a vicarious way, imagined myself traveling to Greece every time I was in these theatres. It was a temporary escape for me rather than thinking about going back to school on Monday morning.

A common goal of the Greek immigrants was to stay for five years, make as much money as possible, and then return to their beloved towns and villages. This my mother could accept. This she could tolerate. After all, five years weren't that great a sacrifice. All of this changed one day when she invited a close friend of hers, Mrs. Margo Theodosakis, over to our house for lunch.

My mother confided in her when it came to the difficult period of adjustment.

"Margo, I'm so happy we can get together once in a while."

"I am too," Margo said. "It's so nice to see you, Anna."

"I'm not that sad anymore," my mother admitted.

"That's good, Anna. You'll get used to it," Margo said in a gentle manner.

"Five years isn't that long. I can do it."

"Five years?" Mrs. Theodosakis looked at her in amazement. "Who told you that?"

"That's what everyone says," my mother said with a trace of nervousness in her voice.

"Anna, do you believe that?"

"Yes, Margo, why shouldn't I believe it?"

"Anna, let me set you straight. They all say that in the beginning, but it's not true."

"Are you sure?" my mother asked.

Margo's words hit her like a bolt of lightning. Her stomach turned upside down. It was a jolt to her system she couldn't bear. She was becoming more upset by the minute.

"I hate to admit it, but it's not true," Margo sadly told her. "Once they become established here with their businesses, it is very difficult to leave. First, it's five years, then six years, then ten and twenty years. There's no end to it. Get used to it and don't fool yourself."

She gave my mother one last piece of advice. "Anna, you must take driving lessons and learn how to drive a car. Without it, you will be lost. It is the most important thing you can do for yourself right now. Do it as soon as possible."

This conversation would remain with my mother for the rest of her life. She was very disillusioned at the impending reality that she would never see her family again.

DO UNTO OTHERS

My mother was one of the most unselfish individuals I have ever known. She was a giving person. If a tenant in the building where we lived had a problem, she was always willing to help in any way she could. Many of them were invited to our kitchen and treated to coffee and pastry. Blanche and Tom Spear, who lived on the second-floor rear apartment, came down almost every day for "tea time," although tea was hardly ever served in place of coffee. Tom Spear was an immigrant from Corinth and worked for my uncle Alex at the 26th Street location back in the old days. The Spears were a wonderful couple.

Their son, Michael, and my brother, John, would wrestle almost every time they met. Sometimes, this battle of the warriors would take place on Mike's bed. They would each have each other in a headlock and would roll from one end of the bed to the other. When they reached the edge, they would somehow maneuver themselves back toward the middle.

A few times they went crashing down to the floor. I used to enjoy watching them. They were so intense you thought they were going to hurt each other badly, but when Blanche yelled out, "Boys, lunch is ready," they immediately let go of each other and rushed over to the kitchen table. It always took about three seconds.

George, our mailman for many years, was a guy who

always had a smile on his face. He was a man who had a positive disposition if there ever was one. On many days, especially during the frigid winter months, my mother would invite him in for coffee, pastry, and an occasional shot of *Metaxa*, which did wonders to warm him up before venturing back out in the cold. He was very appreciative to say the least. Everybody liked George. He was the best mailman we ever had.

At the dinner table I had an insatiable appetite. I always wanted more food. Most of the time, there was plenty of extra portions to go around. If there wasn't, my mother solved the problem in her own unique way.

"Mom, is there any more food left?"

She knew there wasn't any.

"Here—take mine," she said.

"No, I don't want to take yours. You eat it."

"No, no, I don't want it. You can have it."

"I can't take yours. That's not right."

"I'm not hungry," she would say as she put more food on my plate. "I've had enough."

To put an end to the debate, she would immediately get up and start cleaning the table. She knew how to diffuse the situation and was pleased that I continued eating. This happened more times than I care to remember.

One of my favorite Saturday morning journeys was when my mother would take me downtown on the elevated (the "L") train. The Oak Park Avenue station was an old wooden frame building with a heater placed in the middle for cold winter days. When the train was approaching downtown Chicago, it would start its upward incline and make me slightly fearful of looking straight down.

We would shop for several hours, and she always bought something for me—a new shirt, a pair of gloves or a Daniel

Boone coonskin hat I had asked for. Our day always ended at the Stop & Shop Café, where we had lunch. It was a treat for both of us. The day I recall more than any other was the day I asked her to take me to a movie. *To Hell and Back,* the World War II film starring Audie Murphy, was released the prior week and I definitely wanted to see it. All of my friends and I craved watching war movies. When I asked her, she didn't hesitate for a moment? *"Pame"* (let's go), she said with a smile on her face.

I knew very well she had no interest in war movies. How she sat through all of those battle scenes without saying a word, I'll never know. She preferred romantic pictures, but she sat through a little more than two hours with me at the United Artists Theatre just to please me.

She also took me to see Little Oscar when he made an appearance in his Oscar mobile. It was at a Jewel food store across the street from our candy store. What a thrill it was when he popped open the door and came out to wave at all the kids who surrounded him. I wanted to get close to him, but it was impossible.

One early spring morning in 1989, my brother John and I found my mother on the floor next to her bed. We didn't know it at the time, but she had suffered a stroke. She was in her late eighties at the time. I tried to pull her up and onto the bed while John was calling the paramedics. With her face and hands trembling, she looked directly at me and said, "Don't try to lift me. You'll hurt your back." I told her not to worry about it and continued to move her to the bed. She must have been feeling moments of fright and shock, but her first thoughts were of me and my safety and well-being.

CONVALESCENCE

My mother spent seven weeks at MacNeal Hospital and had therapy every morning and every afternoon. The only time off for her were Sunday afternoons. She recovered in a short period of time due to the hospital's excellent physical therapy division.

She maintained her sense of humor even while convalescing in a hospital bed. Her doctor came into her room one morning accompanied by two nurses and several medical student interns from the University of Chicago. The students brought their notebooks and pens to document what she was going to say, if anything. My sister Pauline and I waited alongside our mother's bed with nervous anticipation. The doctor presented a scenario to see if she could comprehend what he was describing:

"Anna, pretend you are back home waiting for friends to come to dinner. You are cooking a roast in the oven, but it has been badly burned and is not suitable to eat. Your guests will arrive in about ten minutes, but you have nothing to give them. What are you going to do?"

Everyone looked at her in anticipation of what she was going to say. The anxious interns had their pens ready. They stared at her, waiting for her response. My mother looked at every one of them as if she were studying human behavior for a psychology class. She glanced over at Pauline and me and then turned her head and stared directly at the doctor.

She tilted her head upward and opened her mouth to talk.

"Big deal," she said. "Call for pizza!"

Everyone burst out laughing and told her how pleased they were that she understood everything. Then she glanced over at Pauline and me and, with a dumbfounded expression on her face, said in Greek so the others couldn't understand, "They are supposed to be intelligent people, but they ask stupid questions." She smiled. We knew she would be on her way to recovery.

After seven weeks of therapy, she was happy to be home. A nurse named Joan came to see her at least twice a week. Joan was very pleasant and had a genuine personality, and my mother liked her very much. On one such occasion I showed her into the house, and the conversation with my mother began.

"Hi, Joanie pony."

"Hi, Anna banana. How are you today?"

"I'm all right. What are we going to do today?"

"We're going to have fun today, Anna."

"Really? What are we going to do?"

"Well, first I have to take a blood test."

"Again? We had a blood test just a few days ago."

"I know, Anna, but the doctor wants another one."

"The doctor has gone crazy with blood tests."

"I know, but what can we do?"

"Can't you take Al's blood instead?"

"No, I'm afraid not."

"Why don't you give the doctor a blood test and see if he likes it?"

"That would be difficult to do, Anna."

"First, he took away my chocolates, and now he's taking away my blood. It's terrible getting old."

I was feeling quite sorry for her, so I gave her a piece

of Hershey's chocolate when the nurse left. Knowing how she hated blood tests, I wanted to cheer her up after her ordeal. She watched me carefully as I slowly peeled off the wrapping and put the chocolate in her hand. She popped it into her mouth and savored every moment. She was happy again.

CAMARADERIE

We didn't have many relatives in Chicago, or in the United States, for that matter. My father had a niece in St. Catharines, Ontario, Canada, and a nephew in Hamilton, Ontario. He also had three uncles in the city—the Loumos Brothers. One of them was Dr. Sarantos Loumos, who had an office downtown. He was a captain in the Greek Army Medical Corps before immigrating to the United States. I was eleven years old when he died.

I still remember an article in the newspaper describing how he passed away of a heart attack while traveling to our house for dinner. I recall looking at the special meal that would have been his. He was a chain-smoker who literally lit each cigarette with the one he just finished smoking. He must have had braces on his teeth because I could hear a clicking sound most of the time when he spoke.

I have fond memories of his brother, Stathis, because he always brought me Hershey's chocolates that he bought on the "L" platform waiting for the train to our house. I knew before he arrived each time that he had a treat for me. He flashed a smile every time he handed me the chocolates. He knew how delighted I was to get them. The brothers always wore suits, vests, and ties when they came for dinner. They were traditional-looking gentlemen and always looked sharp. Sadly, I was too young to know them very well.

The Greeks had their own support groups. They were not only friends but they had a type of networking framework and would help one another whenever there was a need. I believe this was the case with most immigrant families. Who else could they rely on? I never fully realized why all of my parents' friends were Greek until I was older.

My mother and father had many friends in the Chicago area they would often visit. The Brachou, Coulolias, Andreou, Demeur, Vames, Colias and Katzourakis families would also come to our house for coffee and pastries. This is how I met my friends Jimmy Demeur, Angelo Siaperas, Alkie Coulolias, and Jimmy Andreou.

My mother made all kinds of pastries to serve to friends when they came to visit. One of my favorites was the *koulouri.* These were oblong pastries with lots of butter. Every time she made a fresh batch, I would end up eating at least five or six at a time. I wouldn't stop there. Within a few hours I would go back and have a few more. She always told me to save some for the guests, but her words didn't faze me. She finally resorted to hiding them. At first, I could not find them, but after a while and after hours of searching, I finally discovered her hiding place. It was a top shelf in one of the closets where she thought they would be out of sight. When I came into the kitchen one afternoon munching on a *koulouri,* she realized I made a unique discovery. Instead of getting mad, she broke out laughing. "I see the little mouse has found the *koulouri*! Such a bad boy," she said as she continued with her laughter.

On a Saturday afternoon in autumn, she took me with her to visit her friend Pota Brachou, who lived on Gunnison Street on the North Side. I think I was about eight years old. She explained what she expected of my behavior before we arrived.

"If Thea Potitsa offers you a piece of cake, that's fine, but don't end up eating the whole cake."

"No, I won't do that. I promise."

After the ladies chatted a while, Mrs. Brachou invited us to the dining room table for some fruit, coffee and, of course, a beautiful-looking cake topped with strawberries, almonds, and whipped cream. What a sight it was. I couldn't wait to eat it; my mouth was watering. After I finished my piece, Mrs. Brachou sliced another piece and was about to put it on my plate. I looked at her and told her to wait.

"What's wrong, Aleko? Have another piece." She looked at me and smiled. I smiled back. I glanced over at my mother, and she glared at me and bit her lower lip. Anyone who is Greek knows that this gesture means you did something wrong or you were committing a shameful act. I looked back at her with a deep frown written all across my face. I wanted that second piece.

"Go ahead, my boy. It's yours." Mrs. Brachou kept smiling. I smiled back at her. I looked at my mother and, lo and behold, she gave me the lip service once again. My smile turned to a frown in less than one second. I looked again at the piece of cake she was waiting to put on my plate. I wanted it.

"You're a growing boy. I know you must want it."

"One piece is enough, Pota. You should save the rest for your family." My mother was always trying to be as polite as possible.

"There's enough for everybody, Anna."

Mrs. Brachou's statement gave me the reassurance I was longing for. She helped with my decision.

I accepted the second piece, and my mother, of course, gave me the lip routine. I looked directly at her and gave her the same lip service. I really bit my lower lip harder than usual because I was determined to convey the message that I had nothing to be ashamed of. When Thea Pota went into the kitchen to make more coffee, we proceeded to give each other a few extra bites of our lower lips. At the end of our visit, I knew exactly what she would say—"*palio petho*" (bad boy).

My impression of all of my parents' friends is that they were dignified and hardworking people. It was customary for the kids to call the women *Thea* (Aunt) and the men *Theo* (Uncle). Even though they weren't technically related to us, it was a gesture we were taught to show respect. I believe this custom prevailed in most Greek families.

The overwhelming majority of our relatives were in Greece. We really missed out on not having them around and not growing up with them. So many of my friends in the Greek community had first cousins who were obviously a part of their extended family. We never experienced this joy. It would have made our lives more fulfilling.

My mother and father on their wedding day

Ready to get started

With my pal Freddy Starr

Pauline and John at the 13th Street prairie

John and Pauline at the store yard

My mother and father at the store yard

My mother among the trees

Pauline, my father and John

Uncle Alex and my father at the ice cream parlor

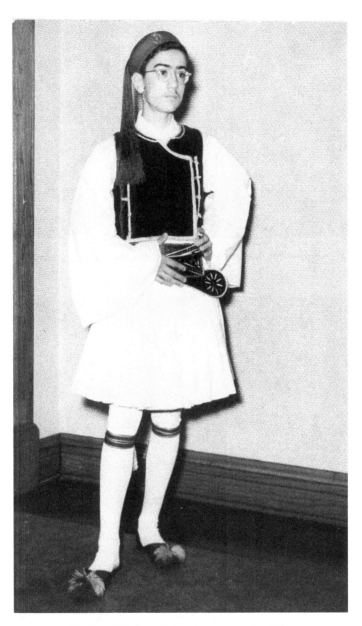

Brother John ready to give a speech at the Greek Independence Day Celebration

Left to right: Pauline, mom, Uncle George, Uncle George Kranios, and John

The little drummer boy

Morton West High School, Class of 1964.

At the Sts. Constantine and Helen Cotilion

At a college dance

Graduation Day at Elmhurst College, 1969.

A happy smile

My father, Blanche Spear and my mother at my graduation

With my mother

With my aunts Phaedra, Maria and Matoula in Greece

Pauline during her college years

Paul and Pauline on their wedding day

A happy Couple

Anna, Pauline and Chris

At Camp George. Left to right: John, mom, me, Anna, Paul and Chris

Mom in a solemn moment

Mom and Anna

John on the ski slopes in Michigan

My Godmother, Elaine, me and Aunt Evangeline

Opa!

Anna and Garen's daughter, Nia

My Marta.

Left to Right: John, Paul, Chris, Mom, Anna, Pauline and me.

THE JAIL AND THE WARDEN

Most of the Greek Orthodox churches in Chicago, as well as in the entire United States, had their own schools. We attended services at the Assumption Church, located on Central Avenue and Harrison Streets on the West Side.

We all attended the Plato School afternoon sessions on Mondays, Wednesdays, and Fridays to learn Greek. Plato also offered an all-day, full-time curriculum on all subjects, which included the study of the Greek language. Classes began at four in the afternoon and ended at six. My father took me and the Andrews brothers—Nick, Jimmy, and Emanuel—who lived about seven blocks from us.

He would pick me up first from Custer Elementary, and I was always worried that the teacher would make the class stay after school and that my father would be waiting in the car and wondering what was happening. I didn't want anyone to know I was taking lessons in a foreign language, so I hid my books under my coat. My real problem was that none of my classmates, to my knowledge, were going to an afternoon school to learn another language. Once again, I wanted to be like everyone else.

None of us wanted to go. We would have preferred to play baseball or be with our friends. On occasion, my father and I would have to go looking for the Andrews brothers in the direction of their school. They either took their time in getting home or they were hiding, hoping my father wouldn't see them. Most of the time, however, they waited patiently on the side of their home. They knew it was a hopeless situation.

Mr. Athanasopoulos gave us a homework assignment at the end of each class. He would give us a page out of our textbooks and tell us to practice reading it at home. How quickly you read it next time in class would show him how much you practiced at home. Everyone had their turn to stand next to him and read the page that was assigned. When Nick got up to read, he would stumble over the second, fourth, sixth words, and so on. The teacher would read faster than Nick. He finally had had enough. It was obvious Nick didn't spend much time practicing at home.

"Katse hamou, katse hamou." (sit down, sit down)

"Why—what's wrong?"

"You didn't study."

"I did," Nick shot back.

"Dropi sou." (you should be ashamed of yourself)

Nick started to walk back to his seat when all of a sudden, he turned around and stared directly at Mr. Athanasopoulos. The teacher stood up and stared directly back at Nick. This continued for at least thirty seconds or so. The entire class was intrigued as to what would happen next. Who would be the first to back down? We thought Nick showed a little bravado by confronting our teacher.

We waited with deep interest. Nothing like this had ever happened before. Greek school was getting to be an exciting place. Finally, Nick looked at the class and declared: "Gee whiz, what a grouch." We all laughed. He then went back to his seat and sat down. The battle of the ages was over.

To get to Plato, my father drove through meandering Jackson Boulevard in Columbus Park. One time Jimmy tried to convince my father to change his mind about taking us.

"Mr. Rassogianis, we don't feel like going to class today. Can you drop us off in the park?"

"No, no. You boys have to go to school."

"Can't you leave us here just this one time?"

"You need to learn Greek. How can you learn anything if you don't go to school?"

"The teacher doesn't like us anyway," Nick answered back.

"I don't believe it. He likes all of you, I'm sure." My father was not one to be swayed.

"Plato School is the jail, and Mr. Athanasopoulos is the warden," Jimmy declared.

Many of the boys would ditch Greek school, and some got away with it. The method they used was very simple. They would wave goodbye to their fathers from the front door of the school, and once they saw them drive away, they ran across the street to Columbus Park. A more common practice was to go to class but come in late. I used this method myself. Sometimes I just hated being there. Taking a few minutes off the clock seemed to alleviate the pain.

Once we were in class, Mr. Athanasopoulos had total control. Nobody got away with misbehavior. On one occasion, two boys in the back of the class were passing notes to each other and snickering about it. They thought they pulled one over on our instructor. He walked to the back and grabbed the note away from one of them and declared: "You are one sly fox—I am one hundred sly foxes."

On a Monday afternoon we were learning what was perhaps the most important document in the Greek Orthodox Church—the Creed.

"Today is Monday. When you come back on Wednesday, you will recite the Creed in Greek by heart."

"What?"

"Are you sure about that?"

We were all unified in our protest. Moans and groans were plenty.

"Don't complain. You can do it," he declared, while looking directly at his class.

"That means we have tonight and tomorrow night only to learn it?" One girl said exactly what all of us were thinking.

"You can do it," he repeated.

When class ended at six o'clock, we gathered outside in the playground and complained to one another while we waited for our fathers to pick us up.

"I won't be able to do it," said Andy.

"I don't think it's fair," said Christina, who everyone knew was an A student.

"I hope he is joking," another girl remarked.

"You know he doesn't joke around, don't you? We're in for trouble for sure," Andy said.

"We're going to tell our parents to skip American school tomorrow so we have time to learn the Creed." This girl offered a solution to the problem.

"They'll never buy it!" a girl named Anastasia cautioned all of us.

All our fathers drove up and parked in front of the school. By 6:05 we were all on our way home to eat dinner. I told my father right away that I didn't want to go to Greek school on Wednesday. He asked me why, and I told him what the situation was.

"I don't think he was serious when he asked the class to do that."

"How do you know?" I was upset.

"Don't worry about it, Ali."

"Can you call him and tell him to ease up on us?"

"I can't tell him how to do his job, can I?"

"But you know him. You are friends. He won't mind it, I'm sure." I tried to plead with my father, but deep down in my stomach, I knew I was wasting my time.

"It's too difficult to learn in two days. He can't be serious. Very few could do it. Do the best you can and learn some of it." He tried his best to keep me calm.

He alleviated my stress for at least a few minutes. My mother had chicken pilaf when we got home, and it certainly pleased me for quite a while. It was one of my favorite meals, and I wasn't worried for at least an hour or so. I couldn't stop thinking about it all night long.

When Wednesday arrived, all the students reluctantly filed into class. Strange as it seems, no one was absent or tardy. We waited quietly for the teacher to arrive. He walked in and stared at all of us for a couple of seconds. We knew right then we were in for trouble. The first thing he said shocked everyone.

"We are going to write a composition in Greek today. Take out your tablets and a pen."

I was wondering whether he forgot about the Creed, and I'm sure my fellow classmates were pondering the same question. We gladly took out a sheet of paper and were ready for his instructions. He wanted us to write at least two pages on a person we believed to be the most influential in our lives. I was never so happy to do an assignment as this one. I hoped it meant that we would not be expected to recite the Creed.

After class some of the students gathered outside and tried to figure out why he never mentioned the Creed. We knew he was too intelligent to forget about it and that the answer must lie somewhere else. Perhaps he just gave us a break from the goodness of his heart. Sometimes happiness arrives in strange ways.

Mr. Athanasopoulos gave private lessons to a brother and sister named Amy and Jimmy, who lived relatively close to the church. He went to their home once a week and taught them in a private room so they would not be disturbed. On one of these occasions, their parents telephoned him that they would be gone for most of that evening, but they reassured him that their son and daughter would be ready for their Greek lessons.

Amy and Jimmy had other plans. When their parents left, they decided to cop out of their lesson. When Mr. Athanasopoulos rang the front doorbell, they did not answer. In fact, they were hiding under the dining room table for fear he might peek through the window. He knocked on the door a few times and then rang the doorbell. They did not answer.

"I know you are there," he shouted.

There was still no answer.

"Open the door. I know you are there."

Once again there was no answer.

"You must open the door immediately and let me in. You cannot get away with this behavior."

Amy and Jimmy started to worry. They came to realize that he meant business. If he didn't leave after all this time—then he would most likely stay until their parents got home. That would have been the worst scenario. They just couldn't take a chance. They crawled out from under the dining room table and reluctantly opened the door. There were certainly quite a few incidents involving Mr. Athanasopoulos, but, in retrospect, he was a very effective teacher, and I learned quite a bit from him.

My brother, John, had a Greek teacher named Iphigenia Cordoyiannis. Apparently, she was a strict disciplinarian and wouldn't allow her students to fall behind in their homework assignments. She was a demanding instructor, as were most of the teachers at Plato. One afternoon John had to use the bathroom and went up to the teacher's desk to ask her for permission. Not wanting the class to hear his request, he whispered in her ear.

"Mrs. Cordoyiannis, may I please go to the bathroom?"

Apparently, she didn't hear him. She was talking to one of the girls in class.

"Mrs. Cordoyiannis, I have to use the bathroom." This time he really meant it, and everyone could sense the determination in his voice.

"Mrs. Cordoyiannis, I have to use the bathroom."

She looked directly at John and with a dumbfounded expression said:

"Such a big boy like you?"

"Yes, yes."

She pointed to the door and told him to go and not take too much time.

After many years of teaching, she became principal of Plato School. One of the stories that circulated about her took place on a cold winter day. It had snowed all week and there was ice everywhere. Mrs. Cordoyiannis ran out of cigarettes and sent a student named Nick Kallas across the street to the restaurant to buy a pack for her. Nick Kallas, by the way, became one of our scoutmasters many years later.

Anyway, she waited patiently for a long time, but Nick still hadn't returned with the cigarettes. Growing more frustrated by the minute, she decided to go across the street and find out what happened. She was obviously very angry by this time.

The restaurant owner told her that Nick bought the cigarettes some time ago and left. She asked where he went, and the owner said he believed Nick went across the street to Columbus Park. Mrs. Cordoyiannis chased after him. She crossed Central Avenue and headed for the lagoon. She spotted Nick on the other side. Apparently, he wanted to kill some time before heading back to class. He couldn't believe she went to the park looking for him. *"Palio pedo (bad boy).* What are you doing here?"

She waved at Nick to come around the lagoon. Nick was taking his time doing it. She grew impatient and couldn't wait any longer. It had been a long time since she'd had a cigarette, and she was obviously having a nicotine fit.

"Wait there. I'll come to you. Don't move," she yelled out to him. Nick was apprehensive when he watched Mrs. Cordoyiannis walk slowly over the frozen lagoon. He couldn't believe what he was seeing. A middle-aged woman walking on ice was not something you see every day. She took a step and then another one. After about four mini-steps, she fell into the water. It wasn't that deep, but it was obviously a shock to her and Nick alike. He knew he would be in trouble. She got wet, angry, and frustrated, but Nick got something worse—a suspension!

THE MICHIGAN WONDERLAND

The Stevensville-St. Joseph area was popular with many Greek families, most of whom were from the Chicago area. My sister Pauline's godmother, Mrs. Athena Siaperas, was the one who recommended it to my parents because she and her husband had been going there for several years. Almost all of us stayed in resorts in the early days, and there were plenty of them up and down the Lake Michigan shoreline. Emil Tosi, who was from Cicero, Illinois, had a restaurant and some cabins on Ridge Road so the Italian families could come up and spend several weeks during July and August. His restaurant became one of the best in the area (and still is).

We first stayed at the Riviera Resort, which was directly across the street from Tosi's. There were summer cabins that formed a circle around a courtyard and a restaurant-cafeteria located at the west end. You always knew when a car entered the area because of the sound of the tires rolling across the stones and pebbles.

I knew when a Buick entered the resort because of the distinctive portholes that adorned the front of both sides. My brother, John, told me that I yelled out, "Boo-ick, Boo-ick." Since the Riviera was located on the west side of Ridge Road, there was a path that led all the way to the beach. It was a prime location.

The Dritsas family, from Chicago's South Side, including

their daughters, were our next-door neighbors. Other friends of ours at the Riviera were the Bays family, also from the South Side, and their children, Alice (Aliki) and Sam (Sotiris). Mr. and Mrs. Georgulis from Chicago's Austin district, and their four daughters, Helen, Vaso, Cleo, and Jo Anne, also stayed at the Riviera.

Years later we stayed at Clamor Court on Glenlord Road. Mr. and Mrs. Clamor were Italian, like most of the resort owners. I remember the front yard seemed immense and beautiful to me. It had lush green grass, pine trees, and majestic-looking Colorado blue spruce. Mr. Clamor had a beautiful, white-framed home at the edge of the courtyard and, of course, it was much larger that the visitors' cottages. I was fascinated by it, but I never went inside.

We had a small cabin that consisted of one main room and a kitchen. We all slept in one room. To say it was too small would be an understatement. I don't know how all of us could be inside at the same time. The fee was $300 for the entire season of July and August. My father and my uncles were working at our candy store and would take turns coming up to see us. For them, it was a break from the long hours of operating a candy and ice-cream business.

We lived next door to an Italian family named Peruccini, who were from Chicago's South Side. They had a son named Richard and a daughter named Yvonne. She became the first love of my life when we were both three or four years old. She was a little chubby girl with curly blonde hair. Actually, both of us had mini potbellies. John has told me that I could never pronounce the name Yvonne, so I used to call her Bun. He said I would go up to her window and cry out in an act of desperation, "Bun! Bun! Bun!"

She, in turn, would run up to her window, look at me, and yell back to me in Italian, "Bambino! Bambino! Bambino!"

The scene was straight out of *Romeo and Juliet.*

There was a boy at the resort named Peter Otis who had the reputation of being a troublemaker. We were not exactly angels ourselves, but with Peter, the tagline kind of stuck. There was an Italian family from Cicero staying at the court, and they had two children named Vivian and Danny. Danny was a chubby and jovial kid who always had a smile on his face. He was one of the friendliest individuals I ever knew, and everyone liked him.

As strange as it may sound, little Vivian used to lick the bottom of her shoes and then go around and brag about it. She even had a little song to accompany her habit: "I'm licking my shoes and you're not." One day, Peter stole Vivian's shoes, twirled them around for a little bit like a cowboy handling a lasso, and then threw them up on old man Clamor's roof. Her parents, needless to say, were not pleased. I think they went out looking for him. Peter suddenly disappeared.

My brother also told me that he heard Peter had thrown a bottle of ink at the outdoor theatre screen at night—right in the middle of a movie. We still don't believe this was true, but it was fun talking about it. I can imagine hundreds of people honking their horns and yelling out of their car windows. It would have been pure pandemonium.

Mr. Clamor had a sweet little canary named Bo Bo, who would follow him all the way to St. Joseph, which was at least a twenty-five-minute ride, and then back home again. Nobody could figure that one out. Mr. Clamor loved his bird very much, and everyone could see why. Unfortunately, our cat, Sugar, attacked and killed it one day, and Mr. Clamor was heartbroken. His beloved Bo Bo was gone for good. He set out to search the entire resort for Sugar, and we thought of all kinds of ways to hide and protect her.

"Where is that damn cat?" he shouted angrily. "I'm going to kill her!"

I don't know how we did it, but we succeeded in hiding her from the wrath of Mr. Clamor. The next day he placed a sign on one of the large maple trees at the entrance to the courtyard on Glenlord Road. It's obvious as to what it was intended for. In big, bold letters, so there would be no doubt as to the way he felt, it read *No Pets Allowed.*

HOME SWEET HOME

After several years of staying at resorts, my father bought five acres of land and had a home built. It had a spacious living room, a full-sized kitchen, three bedrooms, an attic, and a large basement. The walls were made of knotty pine wood, and it really resembled a summer home.

There was a certain country pine scent in the air every time we walked in the house. It had a prime location and was only blocks away from Glenlord Beach on Lake Michigan. We had plenty of fruit trees, including pear and cherry. Far in the back of the house, we had grapevines and even some blackberry bushes.

By giving us a summer home, my father not only enabled us to enjoy the beaches and the warm weather, but he also created a different perspective on life for us. It gave us the opportunity to escape from the city environment and the stifling urban summer heat and exchange it for open air, beautiful forests, and a certain sense of physical and mental freedom. It was a clean break from the drudgery and responsibilities of work and school. It was a chance to get acquainted with new people and develop interesting friendships. Some of these would last a lifetime.

At the southwest corner of our property on Ridge Road, there were two tall oak trees. They must have been seventy or eighty years old. They were huge, beautifully structured, and had willowy hanging branches which were long and wide. They looked like they belonged on a Southern plantation much like Three Oaks in the movie *Gone with the Wind*.

My father decided to put up a swing on the tree that was farthest from the house. I don't know if he bought it from the Stevensville hardware store or if he put it together himself. If he constructed it himself, it was a creative piece of work. It was a wide and very sturdy piece of wood, and the ropes were thick and tight. There was nothing flimsy about it, that's for sure.

When it was finally ready, my brother and sister and I took turns getting on. The first time I tried, I was a little frightened. I was seven or eight years old, and I remember being apprehensive about it. I held on tight to the ropes, as tight as I possibly could. Deep down, I knew my father wouldn't let us get on the swing if it wasn't safe, but I worried about it anyway.

Sometimes my father would push me a little too hard, and there would be a break in the swing at its highest level. I always thought it was so high that I would be touching the leaves on the tree, but I never did. I knew he was watching me every minute. As the days went by, I gained more confidence.

"Push me higher, Pa."

"No, no—it's high enough," he would shout back to me.

"Aw, come on, a little higher." I was getting bold.

"Haven't you had enough for a while?"

"No, I want to go up and touch the tree again."

"All right. Be very careful." He always wanted to make me happy.

I came to enjoy it more and more. If there was a day we didn't go to the swing, I was disappointed.

"Are we going to the swing today?" I could be a pest very easily.

"Again? We went yesterday."

"I know, but I like it." I wouldn't take no for an answer.

"All right, but just for a little while."

I guess he figured it was easier to take me than hear me complain all day.

The tree with the swing brought so much pleasure, but it also brought tragedy and sadness to all of us, especially to my brother, my sister, and me. We had a wonderful cat that year named Jinny, and we brought her with us to Michigan. She was the daughter of our other cat, Sugar. One afternoon our family was visiting friends somewhere in the area. The day turned nasty when it became very windy and started to rain. There was thunder and lightning everywhere.

Obviously, visibility was extremely poor, and my father was very cautious and slowed down considerably on the way home. When we returned, he pulled his Mercury into our driveway and parked it as close to the house as possible. We looked all around for Jinny to bring her into the house, but we couldn't find her. We kept yelling, "Jinny, Jinny," but to no avail. We thought she most likely found refuge under a bench or chair on the rear patio. The storm was too harsh to continue the search.

The next morning, we looked out the window to see if she was there.

"I can't see her anywhere," said John.

"Maybe she's up in a tree and afraid to come down," added Pauline.

"Let's go outside and find her," John told everyone.

My mother told us not to worry because cats have a way of knowing what to do to survive bad weather.

Her words of encouragement did not subdue our apprehension. We were sick with worry. Pauline searched in back of the house, and I looked on the north and south sides. John went in front and on the road. There was no trace of her, and there wasn't much we could do. Since the grounds were completely saturated with water, we stopped looking.

The following day we walked over to the swing with my father. He promised he was going to spend some extra time with us, and we were excited. As we got closer, John noticed something in the tall weeds. It was black. We ran over to him and stared down at the ground.

"Jinny, Jinny," Pauline and I cried out.

John just kept staring at Jinny's lifeless body. My father went back to the house and got a shovel from the basement. He came back and buried little Jinny. The rest of us just couldn't bear to watch this morbid process and returned to the house. My mother tried her best to console us. It was one of the worst days we ever had.

I remember someone saying that Jinny was up on a telephone wire and was struck by lightning and died immediately. I don't know who said this and I still don't know if it was true. Besides, how would anyone know? It was dark and pouring rain; the visibility was very poor. This story was repeated many times over the years, and I guess it stuck with all of us.

It was always cooler under the trees than it was anywhere else, and each time I went up on the swing, I could feel the breeze brushing adamantly against both sides of my face. I felt much like a bird flying unrestrained in the bright sky and roaming freely among the clouds. The coolness was absolutely wonderful.

I don't know where my father got the strength to push us for so many hours, day after day, but he never let up. I think that part of the reason was that, during those years of the early 1950s, he was as happy as he could be. His life was finally taking shape after many years of serving in the Greek Army during the Balkan Wars and working long hours so many years at our ice-cream parlor and candy stores in Chicago and Berwyn. He came to the United States after being discharged from the Army to help his father and his two brothers—my uncle Alex and Uncle George. He endured many years of hardship and sacrifice without much relief.

He loved being in Michigan just as much as we did, and it showed. Every time he would give me a hearty push on the swing, he yelled out, "Opa, opa." I often looked back at him to see his reaction, and there was always a smile on his face. I knew he was a blissful soul. It made me happy too.

I guess you could say we were both in a very contented period of our lives. He created a family, had success in a difficult business venture with his brothers, and built a summer dream home in beautiful southwestern Michigan. As I look back, it seems as though that period for him was as good as it gets—or at least very close to it. Many years later he would have periodic phases of depression. I don't know if it was delayed reaction from his days in the war, but he suffered miserably from it—and so did all of us.

Of course, being a kid, I had no responsibility and was only concerned with going to the beach every day and going "hunting" in the prairie with my friends Jimmy and Angelo. When I was on that swing, I felt my father had my back, mentally and physically, and he was being supportive of me in every way.

The swing was a bridge between us, although I never thought of it that way until now. It signified a bond that I trusted would never be broken by either of us. It was strong. It showed that we loved each other, and nothing serious would come between us.

In later years the bond would waver a bit from time to

time. I suppose we both had our differences and wouldn't see eye to eye in many different circumstances. When I grew older, I seemed to drift away from communicating that much with him. There were times I lacked a fondness for him due to reasons I can't even remember the details of today.

Whatever they were, they were minor in scope. Perhaps I thought that his opinions and his philosophy of life were outdated, and I didn't have any desire to hear about them. Now I wish I had sat down with him more and listened to what he had to say.

The fact that I remember the details of him pushing me on that swing during those golden Michigan years means that I will never forget what he meant to me. He did so much for me, and the whole family, during his lifetime.

The tree is gone now, but I'm thinking more about the swing. It connected us. It was something that we both enjoyed and was a vehicle to make us closer as father and son. It will always be a passageway from deep in my heart to his eternal memory.

CAMP GEORGE

My uncle George spent more time in Michigan than anyone else I know. He loved being there, and he took immaculate care of the house and the grounds. We often referred to the property there as Camp George, in his honor. He knew many of the farmers in the area and, needless to say, they got to know him very well also. He was a genuine wheeler-dealer.

He knew how to get the best prices for farm products from all of them. After he would finish buying what he wanted, he would tell everyone a humorous story. They all liked him, even though he told the same old jokes over and over again.

He was a character. He had a select group of friends in the area, including Mr. and Mrs. Mangiantini, a very nice Italian couple who lived across the street, and an Armenian family who had a summer cottage on Glenlord Road near Red Arrow Highway.

Uncle George and my brother John planted more than 500 seedlings, including red, white, and jack pines, on a hill in back of the house in 1954. One year later, John planted more than ten pine trees, including some Colorado blue spruce, in the back and on the side of the Demeur house next door.

Uncle George was also known for his gardens. He grew zucchini plants, tomatoes, and green beans, to name a few, in a large area on the south side of the house. The small leaves from the zucchini plants were perfect for making Greek-style *briami* (vegetable stew) dinners. Nothing tasted better. There was only one problem with Uncle George's garden. He created such a large one that by the middle of August of every year, it became so wild he lost control of it.

He and John also did quite a bit of canning. Most of it was done on our kitchen table. They canned tomatoes, green beans, and pears and almost had a canning industry going for them. John tried to can beets by himself to prove to my uncle that he didn't need any help.

When he was having problems, he sought advice from Ada Stoes, one of our neighbors. Ada, her husband, George, and their son, Manny, lived in Chicago near California Avenue in the Gage Park neighborhood. They moved to Stevensville permanently when her husband retired. John would telephone Ada on the sneak so nobody would know. Ada was a good teacher. If Manny answered the phone when John called, Manny would yell out, "Mom, your student is on the phone." I guess John eventually got the hang of it. I don't know if anyone knew that he had a secret advisor.

George Stoes was one of the most avid White Sox fans I ever knew. Unlike other Greek men in the area, who didn't care much for baseball or perhaps never fully understood it, he had a passion for it. Every time he went to his bedroom for an afternoon nap, we could hear the radio next to his bed broadcasting the ball game. He even came into the living room once in a while to update everyone on the score, even though most of us weren't interested to begin with. When you heard him swearing in Greek or even in English, you could conclude that the Sox had either blown the lead they had or lost the game.

Mr. Stoes used to call me Alec. Once he made a comment

to me that I couldn't quite understand. He said, "Alec, if someone offers you something to eat, never refuse it. Do you know what I mean?"

"Sure, I know," I answered.

I didn't know at the time what he was talking about or why he would make a comment like that. It wasn't until years later that I finally figured it out. I realized that such a statement was attributed directly to his background and the extreme hardship he experienced when he came to this country as a young boy.

He probably worked eighteen or nineteen hours a day at odd jobs and had his share of desperation, as most immigrants did. I'm sure he experienced days in which he had very little, if anything, to eat. Most likely, there were times when he had only a few nickels in his pocket. He not only became a successful businessman, but more importantly, I realized he was also a true pioneer.

George Stoes, however, was a difficult man to please. Having been in the restaurant business for so many years, he certainly was opinionated as to restaurants' quality and overall operation. I recall a conversation John had with him.

"George, what's your favorite restaurant in the area?" John asked.

"I don't have any," he responded.

"Oh, come on, there must be one or two that are better than the others?"

"They're all the same," George insisted.

John pushed the issue, knowing that the answers might humor him. "What about Holly's?" He started a litany of queries he hoped would last for a while.

"Too soggy," George said calmly.

"What about Tosi's?"

"Too greasy," George said.

"What about Schuler's?" John wasn't about to give up.

"They have too many appetizers," George said with a slight frown.

"What about Ritter's?" John was running out of restaurants.

"They cut the meat the wrong way," George said firmly.

"If you had to pick one, which one would it be?" John thought he had him cornered on this one.

"None of them, John." George grinned. That was final.

Everyone also knew that Mr. Stoes didn't like Chicago very much. He disliked the congestion with a passion. He preferred to be in Michigan. The conversation with John shifted to travel.

"How long are you going to stay in Michigan, George?" John asked.

"As long as possible," George declared. "Everybody thinks that when the Labor Day weekend is over, then the summer is over too. That's not true."

"That's a good point, George."

"Why is everybody in such a rush to go back to Chicago?" George asked, perplexed.

"Well, they have to either go back to work or go back to school," John said.

"I don't have to do any of those things, John."

"Why should you go back to Chicago at all?"

"I have to go back to catch a plane to Florida," George admitted.

"That's a good reason." John laughed. "How long will you be in Florida?"

"A few months."

"And then you'll be back to Chicago?" John asked.

"I have to go back, John."

"Why do you have to go back?"

"I have to catch a plane to Greece!" George exclaimed.

John laughed again. I guess there was no doubt about it. George preferred to be anywhere but Chicago.

"Why do you want to go back to Chicago, John?" George asked once again. He still couldn't figure it out.

BADGE OF HONOR

It was six o'clock on a Friday evening. I was so excited to get started that I hurriedly gulped down the chicken and vegetables my mother had prepared for dinner. I told my father that we needed to be careful so we wouldn't be late. He told me not to worry about it. I picked up my duffle bag and put on my winter jacket, and we were on our way to the Assumption Church parking lot on Central Avenue on Chicago's West Side. The scoutmaster told us we were leaving for Tippecanoe, Indiana, at seven o'clock sharp and not a minute later. I can still remember the seriousness of his demeanor when he lectured us a week before:

"We're leaving for Tippecanoe, Indiana, next Friday evening at seven o'clock sharp. We will have four cars taking us there, and I'll let you know whose car you will be assigned to at the end of the meeting tonight. We will be sleeping in cabins that have fireplaces, but you need to bring warm clothing. It gets very cold, especially in the early morning. Does everybody understand that?"

"Yes sir," we all shouted out in unison.

"We will be going on a thirty-five-mile hike the next morning, and you will get a medal for it."

"Yeah, all right!" We cheered as loud as we could.

To have a medal pinned on your uniform was one of the great thrills of being in the Boy Scouts. It was a badge of honor and a source of glowing pride. Every time I put on my uniform, I felt so good about myself. I felt like I was an important part of a respected and admired organization. I felt like I was in an army for young boys.

Another thing we considered to be of the utmost importance was a promotion to assistant patrol leader. You got to wear a whistle attached to a braided red cord that dangled from your left front pocket. When you walked, the whistle would sway back and forth. We thought it was the coolest thing on earth.

The scoutmaster continued with his lecture:

"We're going to meet in front of Plato School at seven o'clock sharp. When I say seven o'clock sharp, I mean seven o'clock sharp."

"Yes sir."

"If you are one minute late, you may as well tell your father to turn his car around and take you back home because we're not waiting for you. Does everyone understand that?"

"Yes sir."

"This is not Greek time. You're not going to come whenever you feel like it. This is the Boy Scouts of America. We do things by the clock."

"Yes sir." Once again, we agreed.

"What time are we leaving?"

"Seven o'clock, sir."

"Seven o'clock what?"

"Seven o'clock sharp."

"That's better."

My father and I arrived a little before seven o'clock, and it looked like everyone was there. We were wrong. One of the four drivers called the scoutmaster and told him he and his son would be late because he needed to pick up his daughter from her ballet class.

The scoutmaster told two scouts, Jimmy and Lucas, to go

to the storage garage, located one block from Plato School, and bring extra blankets and several sleeping bags in case they were needed later. The boys left, but it took them a long time to return. Our leader was getting visibly irritated. He decided to send another two boys, Tom and Peter, to see what happened to Jimmy and Lucas. It was now seven thirty.

Jimmy and Lucas returned and said the supplies were difficult to find because of the abundance of clutter in the garage; otherwise, they would have returned a lot sooner. They didn't see Tom and Peter. The minutes were ticking away. Another driver had called and said his son couldn't find his mess kit for cooking meals. They would be late. It was now eight o'clock. The scoutmaster sent Jimmy and Lucas back to the garage to look for Tom and Peter.

"We're going around in circles," he shouted.

One of the fathers finally arrived and apologized to everyone. It was now eight forty-five. Tom and Peter were back and said they were looking for Jimmy and Lucas inside Plato School. They thought they might be there after failing to find them in the garage. One half hour later, the other father showed up with his son, but said he needed to make a phone call before we left for Tippecanoe. The nearest phone booth was across the street and down the block. The scoutmaster told him to hurry. It was now nine thirty.

There was some confusion regarding car assignments, and it had to be corrected before we left. Also, several of the drivers and scouts were raising issues about the travel arrangements, which turned out to be ridiculous and totally uncalled for. The scoutmaster reviewed his map of Indiana and told the boys one more thing before we got in the cars.

"Remember, everyone, this is the Boy Scouts of America."

"Yes sir."

It was ten o'clock, and we were on our way—-so much for efficiency!

It was almost one thirty in the morning before we arrived at our cabin. It was as cold as could be with a dampness in the air that seemed to penetrate our tired bodies through and through. We selected our double bunk beds as the scoutmaster and two of the fathers brought in some wood to get a fire going. Despite being tired after a long day and a seemingly endless trip, it was thrilling to be on a camping trip.

During each spring, summer, and autumn, we slept in tents, curled up in our sleeping bags in front of a campfire. Obviously, the leaders selected cabins during the winter months, but the boys enjoyed both. In both situations we would freeze in the early morning because the fires would be totally out by then.

In warm weather we cooked our food over the campfire, and the taste was always terrible. By the time we arrived home on a Sunday night, we were starving. In the winter, meals were prepared for us occasionally at a central cabin or lodge, which was more practical and convenient.

Tippecanoe River State Park was a wonderful place. Although there was a strong winter chill in the air, there was mostly sunshine and a clear sky. The river and the surrounding forests were breathtaking. Some of the trees still had a few copper-colored leaves hanging on them with some spots of snow. The ground was clear with the exception of a few patches of ice evenly spread out.

For us, living in the city as we did, it was a perfect getaway. The cabins were old but clean. The fireplace was trimmed with solid brown brick and had an extremely large, open hearth. I guess it was necessary to keep such a large cabin warm throughout the day—and especially during the twilight hours. We found the rustic smell of the old cabins to be exhilarating, and it gave us a strong sense that we were somewhere deep into the woods.

OBEY THE SCOUT MOTTO

Very early Saturday morning at Tippecanoe, the adults were shouting at us to wake up and get out of bed. We had to hurry through breakfast to begin our thirty-five-mile expedition. I can vouch for all of us and say we were definitely shivering at such an early hour with no heat to speak of. Before long, the cross-country hike began.

A scout named John Crisopoulos had a problem with his bootlaces. He tried to tie them, but they kept breaking. John and I told the others to go ahead and that we would catch up. The scoutmaster, visibly anxious to start, told us not to take too much time. Besides, we knew about the layout of the trail because we had detailed maps.

As we tended to John's bootlaces, we noticed a boy hiding in one of the corners near the fireplace. We went over to see who it was. It was Dimitri. He was a heavyset boy, much larger than the others, who didn't really care that much about being a scout. He never tried to elevate himself to the rank of First Class, Star, or Life. After two years he remained a lowly Tenderfoot.

John and I initially thought Dimitri just didn't want to walk thirty-five miles and purposely hid until the others were gone, but it was more than that. He was sick. We didn't know how sick he was. He had the chills and slurred his words while trying to talk. He didn't look good at all.

"Hey, Dimitri, are you all right?" John asked as he placed

his hand on Dimitri's shoulder.

He did not respond.

"Hey, Dimitri, how do you feel?"

"I'm freezing," he finally said.

John looked at me and asked if there were any extra blankets in the cabin.

"I'll go and take a look," I answered.

"Sit a little closer to the fire, Dimitri," John recommended.

"That's a good idea. Help me."

I found a blanket in a pile of supplies and brought it over. He bowed his head as if telling us he just couldn't cope. John got a cup of hot water and found a packet of tea bags in the scoutmaster's personal belongings. He gave a cup of tea to Dimitri.

"Drink this. It will do you some good."

"I don't want it. I can't drink it."

"Give it a try, Dimitri. It will help you." John was persistent.

"All right. I will try it."

"That's a good guy."

John was a good scout. He had recently passed the test for Star, and he deserved it. He always cared about others and tried to help in any way he could. He encouraged the other boys to improve themselves by reading and studying for merit badges, and he had become an assistant patrol leader in the owl patrol a few months earlier. John was a born leader.

The tea didn't help much as Dimitri started groaning and holding his stomach in agony.

"I'm in bad shape, you guys. My insides feel like they're caving in on me."

"Hang on, Dimitri. Hang on." I tried to encourage him, but I didn't know what to say. Once again, he bowed his head.

"Hey, John, we've got to run for help. We can't just sit here and do nothing."

John took me aside so Dimitri couldn't hear what we were saying.

"Listen, Al, I think you're right. What if the worst happens, and we did nothing?"

"We've got to catch up with the others and get the scoutmaster to contact an ambulance and take him to the hospital." I was convinced we had no other choice.

"Let's tell Dimitri," John said.

Dimitri didn't respond that well. He nodded his head a bit but didn't talk. We reassured him that he would recover, but we needed to tell the others just in case. He nodded once more as if giving us his approval.

"We'll be back in a hurry," I shouted.

"That's right," John agreed.

With those final words, we flung open the cabin door and took off. Since we were familiar with the trail, we started running immediately. Our lungs were quickly filling up with cold air as we ran alongside the partially frozen river. Fortunately for us, it wasn't snowing or raining.

About twenty minutes later, we came across an old bridge and stopped dead in our tracks. We had to decide whether to keep following the river or cross it. We were afraid. The bridge was not solid underneath. There were openings every two feet or so, and you could see all the way down to the river.

"What do you think, John? Is it safe?"

"I don't know. I don't really trust it. Do you?"

"Not really, but we have to make a decision."

"We will save a lot of time if we take the bridge. I know for sure," John said.

"I guess we have to do it then. We've got to help Dimitri."

We started to cross the bridge, and it was the most ominous journey either one of us had encountered in our young lives. We were downright petrified as we made our way to the center. We could see the water below us, and it was not pleasant.

The protrusion of the ice upward seemed to convey the message that we made an unfortunate decision. We slowed down as much as we could but kept going. The scouts always taught us to be resourceful in any given predicament we encountered—and we were.

"Don't look down," John shouted out to me.

"I can't help it. If I don't look down, my foot will get caught between the wooden boards."

"I know, I know, but you can't fall down to the river. The most you can do is stumble a little. We've got to keep going."

"I know," I shouted as I stared down at the white mounds of ice that were slowly moving westward on the choppy water. I couldn't help it.

"Keep running, Al. Keep running."

I don't know how much time had gone by at this point, but it seemed like an eternity. I was getting exhausted. The cold air seemed to penetrate my lungs as never before. I felt as though they would burst at any moment.

As soon as we finished crossing the bridge, we fell to the ground in total relief. It was finally over, and we had succeeded. John and I hugged each other as brothers. We were proud to be scouts.

We continued to run. It was easier now that the crossing was finally over. About ten minutes later, we slowed our pace to a jog. It was easier to communicate then.

"Do you realize that we have this entire situation in our hands, Al?"

"What do you mean?"

"I mean that if the worst should come to Dimitri, we might get the blame for it."

"We're doing all we can, John."

"You and I know that, but what will the others think—the other scouts, the scoutmaster, and all the fathers?"

"They might say we didn't run fast enough. They might say we wasted too much time getting started or that we took too many breaks. People will always doubt us, and we will have to live with it. Is that what you're talking about, John?"

"That's exactly what I'm saying. If they blame us, it will be with us for the rest of our lives. We'll be screwed royally, Al."

"What can we do?"

"Let's run faster. We have to."

"Go, go, go," I shouted as loud as I could.

Shortly thereafter we saw something that thrilled us to no end. We were as ecstatic as we could be. In a small section of the forest, among several hundred Colorado blue spruce trees, was the figure of a man wearing a brown hat with a dark leather band around it. He was walking away from us in the opposite direction.

"That guy looks like a park ranger, doesn't he?"

"He sure does, Johnny. Let's not let him get away."

"Hey, hey, hey, hey," we both yelled at the same time and as loud as we could.

"Sir, sir, hey, hey."

The man kept walking in the opposite direction. We knew we had to stop him. Our troop was still too far away for us to reach. This man was our only hope.

"Hey, hey, sir." We wouldn't let up.

We picked up the pace and ran as fast as we could. I don't know where we got the extra energy. Giving up the chase was not an option.

The ranger turned his head slightly to the right. We thought it was a sign that he heard something.

"Please turn around; please turn around," I kept repeating out loud.

"It won't be long, Al. Keep running."

Just then, the ranger turned his head all the way around and saw us. He stopped and started walking in our direction. A sense of sheer joy consumed my mind and my entire body at the same time. Finally, we stopped directly in front of him.

"What are you boys doing? Are you lost?"

"No sir. We are with Troop 360 in Chicago, and one of us is very sick back in our cabin. We were running to catch up with the rest of the boys and our scoutmaster. Can you help us?"

We gave him all of the information regarding the location of our cabin. He telephoned for an ambulance, and shortly thereafter all of us were on our way to save our friend Dimitri. Our scoutmaster was summoned from the trail and made it back to the cabin.

Later that day he commended John and me for what we did. "You boys are true scouts, and I congratulate you. I'm going to recommend both of you for lifesaving medals and citations."

After an overnight stay at a nearby hospital, Dimitri was released. As it turned out, he had a case of the flu and severe stomach cramps. That was why he was in so much pain. He made a full recovery, and all of us were relieved.

About a month passed before we heard from the Boy Scout Council. They congratulated us for adhering to the scout motto of "Be Prepared," but they rejected awarding us the medals because Dimitri was not in a life-or-death situation. It didn't matter to us. We were happy that he was alive and well.

John and I reflected on this incident much later and thought about it from a few different perspectives. Sure, we wanted to help Dimitri. We wanted to do everything possible to assist in getting help to him. We also would have felt extremely guilty if he had died. I'm sure everyone would have said it wasn't our fault, but there may have been talk that we could have done something more. I don't know what that would entail.

I can't imagine what else was in our power to do except to run faster than we did. I don't know if we were capable of that. Perhaps taking the other route would have been more advantageous than crossing the bridge. I don't think so, but it was possible. John and I finally came up with a final thought that we would never forget: perhaps the lives we were running for were our own.

WORKING ON UP

I had my first job when I was a junior in high school. It was handed to me on a silver platter by John Chrisopoulos, my friend from scouts. I can't remember why he didn't want to keep it. It consisted of delivering lenses for an optometrist in Oak Park named Sam, who was Jewish, and an assistant named Tony, who was Italian. They were both nice guys and were very good to me. I would take the Lake Street "L" downtown to Madison Street and drop off lenses to an optometrist there and then return and take the Harlem Avenue bus to Grand Avenue in Chicago and drop off more lenses. I started work after school at 4:00 and would finish by six or six thirty. It was perfect.

Taking the job with Sam and Tony meant giving up extracurricular activities at Morton West, especially athletics, but John did a fine job of convincing me to take it.

"You can make money and have money all the time," he would say.

"What about the time factor, John? Are you sure I won't be working late?"

"No, not a chance. I had the job for two years and I never worked past six."

"I have to make sure I have time to do my homework at night."

"Don't worry about it. You'll have time. Besides, you'll be making money and you won't have to ask your father all the time for spending money. You can take out your girlfriend every weekend."

John was a personable guy and a persuasive salesman. It was sad when he was injured in a sleigh accident in elementary school that cost him the loss of one of his kidneys. He had to be very careful from then on. I was in disbelief when I saw his obituary in the *Chicago Tribune* a few years ago. I went to the funeral and spoke to his mother and a niece.

John died of a heart attack almost instantly while driving his car on the North Side. His mother remembered me even after so many years. His niece made a comment that I haven't forgotten. She said: "It's so nice of you to come after knowing John so long ago. It's so touching that you remember him." I told her that he was a guy I could not forget.

I worked for Continental Airlines at O'Hare Airport every summer for three years, loading and unloading luggage and cleaning and vacuuming the insides of aircrafts. The supervisor was a man they called Binky, and he walked around with a wad of keys dangling from his back pocket. There must have been at least thirty keys of all sizes. We always said that one day his keys would drag him to the ground. It wouldn't really take much to do it because he was super-thin and somewhat uncoordinated. We thought he must be a very important guy to have so many keys.

Continental handled all foreign carriers such as Lufthansa, Air France, and Swiss Air. In addition to handling luggage, we also loaded and unloaded bodies. I still remember how impersonal it made all of us feel when we knew there was once a living human being inside those wooden crates. When we first looked at the boxes, they resembled containers one would store hardware or tools in.

Not all of my summer and afterschool jobs went so well. I took a summer job at the Water Tower Inn on north Michigan Avenue in a swanky part of downtown. I can't remember if I was hired as a waiter or a busboy, but my first day on the job was one I'll never forget. It was awful. Several well-dressed ladies came in and sat at a table by the window. They looked like they were working at a nearby office and, at any rate, they certainly looked very professional.

I was told by the manager, a stern and arrogant middle-aged woman if there ever was one, that the ladies wanted to relax for a while and have tea before ordering lunch. I made four cups of tea and placed them on a tray to carry to the dining room. I walked across the large dining room slowly so as not to make a mess. Just as I approached them, I slipped and the tea spilled all over their table and onto their dresses and the carpeting below. I was stunned. I can still hear their faint cries for help:

"Oh, my God," yelled one.

"Look what you've done!" cried another.

"Can't you look where you're going? Are you blind?"

"I'm terribly sorry, ladies. I tripped and lost my balance," I blurted out with an attempt to justify myself.

"You've ruined our dresses and our lunch," they shouted in unison.

Just then the manager came over and realized what had occurred.

"I'm terribly sorry, ladies. I'll have my help clean this up right away. I'll pay for lunch. Please accept our apology." She tried to do some of the cleaning herself.

By this time, I had gone back to the kitchen area and had taken off my work jacket and was ready to leave. I knew I would be fired. The manager came in and asked me how I could do such a thing, as though I had planned it all along.

"Ma'am, I'm leaving. You don't have to worry about me anymore."

"How careless can you be?" the manager shouted out to me as I exited the restaurant from the back door. She just watched. I walked two blocks or so, and went down the stairs to the subway. I got out of there so fast, she probably didn't have time to fire me. I never heard from the restaurant again and I didn't expect to. When the train came, I found a place by the window and sank my body low on the seat.

I started thinking about what had just occurred, and I wasn't happy about it. I kept telling myself that it wasn't my fault and that I tried to do my best. It didn't help. It was my fault. I should have been extra cautious. I began to think I wasn't capable of holding down a job. What was I going to do in the future—screw up again and again? After a few days I dismissed the entire incident from my mind.

I had a job working on Saturdays at Hale Drug Store on the corner of Oak Park Avenue and North Avenue in Chicago. I took care of the front cash register and made deliveries to customers in the area. It was owned by two Jewish guys named Herb Retsky and Ernie Ernest. I always got a kick out of Ernie's name.

One of their customers was a sickly woman named Mrs. Kenny in Elmwood Park. She was one of the nicest individuals I ever met. She would always give me big tips and say, "Take out your girlfriend," or "Don't worry so much about school. You'll do fine." She would end our meeting with, "Life is too short, so enjoy yourself."

One cold and snowy Saturday morning while on my way to the drug store, I wasn't feeling very well. Perhaps it was the weather or maybe I had a bad week at school. As I entered the store, I was greeted by Herb and he said, "You won't be going to see Mrs. Kenny anymore. She died last night." Although I knew she was very ill, it came as a big blow. The atmosphere at the drug store was depressing all day. I still haven't forgotten the kindness shown to me by Mrs. Kenny. She was one of a kind.

STEP UP TO THE PLATE

My years as a student at Elmhurst College were also during the height of the war in Vietnam. All the boys at school were talking about it. It was difficult to concentrate and do what was expected of us and, at the same time, think about being drafted into the Army. We were all worried about receiving a letter from the government.

I kept trying to push it out of my mind, but the thought would always find its way back. One guy I knew signed up for the Air Force and another with the Coast Guard just to avoid being drafted. One Greek guy told me he thought of going to medical school in Greece. I still remember his words:

"They won't draft you if you're in medical school," he said with an air of confidence.

"Are you sure about that?" I asked.

"Yes. I already checked it out."

"How good are your Greek language skills?"

"I know a little, but overall, they're not that great."

"If that's true, then how can you pass the examinations?"

"I can't," he admitted.

"Then why are you going?"

"I figure it this way. They can't kick me out until the end of the semester, or perhaps the end of the academic year. All that time I'll be protected from the draft."

"So, you're going to go through all of that knowing

you're going to fail and come home?"

"Yeah, that's about right," he admitted.

"I guess you have it all figured out," I told him. I never found out what happened to him.

In the autumn of my junior year, I received a letter that ordered me to take the physical examination for the armed services. I was to report to a location in downtown Chicago on a certain day. The process took up the entire day, and I was informed that I passed. This meant that most likely within a week I would receive a draft notice.

Three days later, to my utter amazement, President Lyndon Johnson issued an Executive Order stating that any student enrolled in a four-year institution would be allowed to finish their degree program. This was great news. By the time I was a senior, the government had initiated a lottery system, meaning that those with the lowest number would be selected first in the draft.

As it turned out, my number was fairly high, and I stopped worrying about it. After graduation, I began teaching and received a deferment. I don't know if it was because I was assigned to a school in Chicago's inner city or whether all teachers qualified regardless of where they taught. I was grateful for it, but later in life I started having a different perspective.

I have often regretted, as a fulfillment of my citizenship, that I did not serve in the military. Why should others serve but not me? Why should others sacrifice at least four years of their young life and not me? It's true that the government was the one that gave me a deferment for teaching, but somehow that kind of logic wasn't good enough for me. I have learned to live with successes and with regrets and to be contented.

SIBLING RIVALRY

A sense of competition usually occurs among brothers and sisters in most families. However, since the three of us were all five years apart, a sense of rivalry never really took hold. Rather than competing with John and Pauline, I took it upon myself to learn as much as I could from their example. Since I was the youngest, I looked up to both of them and was proud of the groundwork they set for me and for themselves. Since both went to college and became teachers, I knew that I had to follow their example and at least go to college. Of course, we had our share of arguments and fights, especially with my brother, but none lasted for very long.

When John was an afternoon student studying Greek at Plato School, he took part in a program at the Austin Town Hall honoring the War of Independence of Greece from the Ottoman Empire. He recited a large portion of a speech, most likely from *A Hymn to Liberty* by renowned poet Dionysios Solomos, and received a thunderous ovation from the audience.

My father convinced John's Greek teacher, Mrs. Cordoyiannis, to shorten the speech a little so John wouldn't be so overwhelmed in trying to memorize it. He did a fine job and we were all very proud. This experience increased his interest in languages as he took four years of Latin in high school and French and Spanish in college.

When I was young, anything I learned about classical music was from John. He would bring home record albums every so often, and I would listen very intently to this sound that was new to me. I soon learned who Mozart, Saint-Saens, and Hayden were, and was able to identify the music with the composer. Kostelanetz, Dimitri Mitropoulos, Bruno Walter, and other conductors became familiar names. After many afternoons of listening to "1812 Overture," "Pathetique," "Capriccio Italien," and "March Slave," Tchaikovsky became my favorite.

Every time I listened to "1812 Overture," I was put in a mild trance. The only other piece of music which had such an effect on me earlier was "Mule Train," by Frankie Laine. I used to stare at the record label going round and round on the turntable and then play it over again when it finished.

When John was in college, I was between the ages of seven and ten. I used to say, "you college boys" to him whenever he came home on weekends. I picked this up from the movie *Mister Roberts.* James Cagney, who played an authoritarian captain of a Navy supply ship during World War II, referred to his officers as "smart-aleck college boy officers." I always got a laugh out of it, and I think John did too.

John was an active member of the Hellenic Professional Society of Illinois. He acted as the program chairman, and it was his responsibility to schedule lectures one or two times a month. It was a demanding job, and he was able to locate mostly Greeks to give presentations to the members. The topics usually focused on history, philosophy, and current events, especially concerning Greece.

He was also an active member in the Greek American Nursing Home Committee to finally build a nursing home in the Chicago area. Most of the other nationalities had their own nursing homes, and it was time for the Hellenic community to achieve this long-awaited goal. It was finally built in Wheeling, northwest of Chicago.

My sister, Pauline, was always watching out for me. She used to take me with her to the movies along with her girlfriends and sometimes just the two of us. When I was in fifth grade, she was a freshman at Morton High School, and she took me to the basketball games. She would sit with her friends, and I would wander all over the place. The jazz band always played at games, and I would stand near them and listen intently.

Those who fascinated me the most were the drummers. I was impressed with their ambidextrous talents and their contribution to the excitement of the evening. These guys were the ones who highly influenced me to take drum lessons at Custer Elementary School, where a student could select any instrument and receive instruction on a weekly basis. The teacher was Mr. Gordon Ludke, who was probably in his mid-forties at the time. He was rather heavyset and had early stages of a receding hairline. He gave all his students a chart which indicated the day and amount of time they devoted to practice at home.

I never practiced as much as he expected, but rather than getting into trouble, I would write in a full amount of time and have my mother initial it. She didn't know what it was all about and never questioned it. I would tell her that she was giving me permission to practice every day. At one of my lessons, Mr. Ludke asked me if I was sure I practiced at home the night before. I had to tell him I did. I'm sure he realized what the truth was. Anyway, I was good enough to be in the concert band. We gave performances at other elementary schools in Berwyn, such as Pershing and Emerson, and it was always exciting to play on a stage in front of an audience.

An attractive girl named Patricia Lawson played clarinet and sat directly across from me at concerts. She was tall and slender with her light brown hair resting gently on her shoulders. She would be looking at her sheet music and then look up at me every time she raised her head. I would smile at her, and she returned the gesture in an alluring sort of way, or at least I thought so.

One time, I missed a couple of snare drum beats because I was distracted by her. Mr. Ludke figured out what was going on. He gave me a foreboding type of glare for a few seconds and it worked. I got the message. He was trying to signal to me to concentrate and pay attention. He wasn't going to look foolish in front of a packed audience because of me. I couldn't blame him.

Parents would help drive the band members to the concerts. I remember on one occasion when a saxophone player named Jerry and I drove in Mrs. Cernota's mini blue Studebaker. It was one of the smallest cars on the road. It almost looked like a car for kids. Both Jerry and Mrs. Cernota were overweight. In fact, they were both fat.

When we reached Pershing School in south Berwyn, both had difficulty in getting out of the car. Both were moaning quietly, while I was trying my best to extract them one at a time. Jerry was sitting in the back seat, which made it more difficult. I couldn't figure out how they got into the car in the first place before they picked me up.

Later in my life I thought I took the wrong instrument. I felt I should have taken anything but drums. It would have been nice to be at home and play the piano or produce the sweet sound of a violin. Even learning Spanish guitar would have been better. You can't exactly listen to a nice melody by banging on drums. Whenever I practiced at home, which was at least four times a week, my mother would say, "Again with the boom, boom, boom?" She had a point.

Pauline, on the other hand, took piano lessons. Her teacher was Mrs. Triner, who lived on Wenonah Avenue, a few blocks from our house. The whole family knew when she was playing when the sweet melodies permeated everywhere. I still remember the standards of "Heart and Soul" and "Misirlou" she played with perfection. After hearing these selections day after day, it's no wonder that I still know the melodies by heart.

Pauline was also a dancer and a prolific choreographer. She was a member of the modern dance club in high school and choreographed a dance number to the music of Harry Belafonte's "Lead Man Holler" before a sold-out crowd at Morton East's historic Chodl Auditorium. There were six girls in her group. Our entire family attended, and we were fortunate enough to find seating in the upper balcony. It was a treat.

My godmother, Elaine, drove down from Evanston to see the performance and be with us. Pauline continued her passion for choreography and dancing while studying education at the University of Illinois in Champaign. Once again, we were there for the performance. The dance number was called "Birthquake," and this time Pauline's group consisted of fifteen girls. It was another stellar performance. We were proud. In later years she would become very active in the Historical Society of Glen Ellyn.

Since my birthday is on August sixth, we always celebrated it at our summer home in Stevensville, Michigan. The organizer of this "main event" of the season was Pauline. She would hang paper plates on the clothesline on the back patio with "Happy Birthday Al" amply displayed across the length of the patio.

Most of the vacationing Greeks in the area would

converge on our house to sing birthday wishes to me. I guess our house was the local hangout. My father would make hamburgers and hot dogs on the charcoal broiler outside, and they were delicious. Everyone brought gifts. I was in my glory. I look back upon all of the things Pauline did for me with fond memories and a deep appreciation.

A ridiculous thing we did growing up was to call people in our building and on the block made-up names. This was all in fun and was certainly nothing vicious or spiteful. Betty Ver Halen, our tenant directly upstairs from us, became Betty Spaghetti. Blanche Spear became Blanche the Avalanche. Her son Mike became Mike the Bike. John the Bomb, Gus the Bus, Joannie Bologna, Anna Banana, Al—Everybody's Pal and Mary Lou the Bossy Shmoo rounded out the rest of the bunch. We had our period of craziness, but it was so much fun.

YOU NEED TO BE INVOLVED

Once in a while, my father wanted me to accompany him when he went to see his tenants for whatever reason. Since his properties included both apartments and businesses, the variety of people he rented to was significant. He would tell me that I needed to be involved and I should know what is going on.

"If the day comes when I am not here, then what are you going to do?" he asked me many times. "You need to know how to handle all of this so you don't lose it."

The scenario usually began this way:

"I'm going down to the Cermak building. Do you want to come along?"

"I don't know" was my usual answer. To be honest I was quite bored every time I went with him and just stood there as he talked to a bunch of older people.

"Come on, let's go. It won't take long."

"All right. I'll come," I would always say reluctantly.

There was an older woman named Lorraine who lived in the first studio apartment upstairs. She was kind and quiet and plainly dressed every time I saw her. I could tell my father liked her and I believe he felt a little sorry for her. Her rent was low and I don't believe he ever raised it.

Down the hall was a man named Richard, whom my father suspected of being an alcoholic and rightly so. After several attempts to reach him over several days, we entered his unit and found him on the living room floor. We called for the ambulance to take him to the hospital, where he was pronounced dead on arrival.

On the first floor was an office which was divided into two sections. One area was occupied by a real estate agent and the other by an attorney. The attorney's name was Edward, and he was very professional and friendly. I took a liking to him right away. One day he told us about his older brother who was serving on a battleship during World War II. The ship was reported missing for quite some time until the Germans admitted that they sunk it in the north Atlantic.

As he spoke about the war, he reached into his left suit coat pocket and pulled out a letter. It definitely looked dated and slightly wrinkled. He opened it and looked at me and my father.

"This is the last letter I received from him before he went missing. I guess he wanted to fulfill his role of being a big brother and give me some advice." Then he read straight from the letter:

I know you will be going into the Army soon and I want you to think very carefully about becoming an officer. It's not all that it's cracked up to be and I hope you'll think it over before you make a decision. It's a thankless job with no rewards. I am telling you from my own experience. Also, whenever you have questions or problems and need someone to talk to, go and ask to meet with the Army Chaplain. You will find that he will be a true friend. Do not hesitate to trust him. I have had a few meetings with my Chaplain and he offered sound advice and comfort.

He folded the letter and placed it back in his pocket. Then he took out a handkerchief from his coat and wiped a tear from his left eye. It appeared as though he kept this letter with him at all times. I realized how close he was with his brother and how much he loved him. I felt sorry for him. On the way home, my father asked me, "Do you see how war can break families apart? Edward's life is not the same since he lost his brother. It's sad, isn't it?" I agreed.

On the other side of town, on Roosevelt Road, my father's tenants in the 1950s included Elsie Borden's School of Dance, Johnny's Italian Beef, and Charley's Tavern. At Johnny's I saw, for the first time, the owner make a beef sandwich on French bread with sweet peppers. The only types of sandwiches I ever saw were the kind we made at home or hamburgers and hot dogs. I was fascinated watching him. When he finished, you could see the juice dripping from both sides. Next door was Charley's Tavern. It wasn't exactly a high-class bar. I remember my father's comments that he made on a typical visit.

"I walk in and right away I find it to be disgusting. One man at the bar looks at another and says, 'You bastard.' The man he was talking to yells back and says very loudly, 'You son of a bitch.' I ask you what kind of language is that? Are these people civilized? I hate it every time I go in there. The owner is a good guy, and I don't want to evict him."

Two doors down from Charley's was a school of dance. The young girls taking lessons looked as decent and as pretty as could be. What a day-and-night difference there was between Elsie's and Charley's and yet, at the same time, they were going about their daily routine in the same structure. They were neighbors.

THE GRECIAN MELODIES HOUR IS ON THE AIR

I never fully appreciated Greek-based music when I was very young. It all sounded too old-fashion and somewhat harsh to my ear. I'm sure I never fully understood it, or perhaps I didn't pay close enough attention. When I was seven or eight, I would watch my uncle Alex sit by the radio and listen to the news. I can still hear the opening announcement: "The Grecian Melodies Hour is on the air. Here is your host, Michael Hatsos."

This, of course, was preceded with three musical chimes to alert the audience as to what was coming. I must say that every time I am in a European airport or even some train stations over there, I hear the exact same melody. It is pleasing to the ear, and it certainly brings back fond memories.

One artist I'll never forget is Sofia Vembo (Bembou). She was the voice of patriotism and victory to the Greek Army during the Italian invasion at the start of World War II and the subsequent occupation by the Axis armies. The most distinct characteristic of her songs was that they portrayed the bravery of the Greek Army by ridiculing Mussolini and the Italian military. Because of her immense contribution to the morale of the people of Greece, the Army awarded her with the rank of major.

She was the Vera Lynn of Greece. One of her most favorite songs was "Paidia Tis Ellados" (Children of Greece). This was sung by everyone during the Greco-Italian War, and from what I have heard from friends and relatives in Greece, it is still popular today and probably will be for a long time to come.

One cold and snowy winter day when I wasn't in the mood to do much of anything, John brought home a record album which completely overwhelmed me. I would play it over and over again. The title was *12 Greek Dances* by Nikos Skalkottas. I was sixteen or seventeen at the time, and it completely changed my outlook toward Greek music and toward the entire Greek culture itself.

Skalkottas composed hundreds of works in his short life, including chamber music, symphonies, and concertos. Societies honoring his name exist in Greece, Germany, and Great Britain. When I mention his name to other Greek Americans, it saddens me to note that relatively few have ever heard of him. It's also interesting that few Greek Americans know anything about current musical artists in Greece.

When I go to a Greek dinner dance or picnic, I hear the same songs I heard thirty years ago. Also, you can guarantee that the blistering cacophony of an extra-loud clarinet will be lodged somewhere in your eardrums for the rest of the evening.

I went to a picnic at the Annunciation Cathedral on La Salle Street several years ago. It used to be one of my favorite outdoor gatherings of every year. I had many friends there, and we would all have souvlaki under the massive tent constructed for the event. There would always be a cool breeze coming from the lake, which made the evening even more enjoyable. Various Greek bands would perform, and we would dance to both Greek and American music. The fun was genuine. Nobody wanted to leave at the end of the evening.

When I went back after many years of absence, I was disappointed, namely with the music. Whenever the band would take breaks, they had a disc-jockey play tapes. Both the band and the tapes were so loud, you had to shout at the person you were talking to in order to be heard. After a half hour of yelling, which is what it was, I left. I never went back. It just wasn't worth it. You go to these events to enjoy yourself and end up being blasted all the way out to LaSalle Street. I have often wondered: *Have any of these people ever heard of Stavros Xarchakos?*

One of my favorite Greek singers is Maria Farantouri. She was discovered by famed composer Mikis Theodorakis when she was only a teenager and performed with his orchestra all over the world. I attended every performance in Chicago. Her rendition of the songs from *The Ballad of Mauthausen* is superb, and when I hear her sing "Sto Perigiali to Kryfo" (The Secret Seashore) I get very emotional. It happens every time.

Other notable favorites for me are Nana Mouskouri's version of "Athena" and Ellie Lambeti singing "Epestrefe" (Turning About) from a composition of Greek poet C.P. Kavafy. It amazes me how the sound of a melody or a specific song can change someone's mood from one instant to the other and bring back a certain time or place in your life that may stand out from all the rest.

IS SHE A GREEK GIRL?

Much has been written about the clannishness of the Greeks, especially among the immigrants themselves. The extent to which this concept has been carried has bordered on the ridiculous. There were instances where family members would not talk to one another because their sons, daughters, brothers, or sisters married Americans. Some families were separated because of this.

When we think about it today, it's almost laughable. I suppose the immigrants felt more comfortable if their children married into other Greek families. They would be more compatible, that's for sure. The successive numbers of generations have changed all of that, and many Greeks are still marrying outside of their ethnicity.

This desire and expectation prevailed in my own family. I remember it vividly. My father would spend a good part of the evenings writing his articles for the *Greek Press* newspaper. He enjoyed it, and it kept him occupied during his retirement years. He received phone calls from all over the country from people who complimented him on his writings. On Saturday night I would walk past him on my way out.

He looked up from his writing duties and asked:
"Are you going out?"
"Yes, I am," I replied.

"Is she a Greek girl?"

"Actually, yes, she is."

I remember his face lighting up like an Edison lightbulb.

"Do you need extra money?"

"No, I think I have enough."

"Are you sure? Here, take some more." He reached into his pocket and pulled out dollar bills and reached across the table to hand them to me.

"Here, take the keys to my car and have a good time."

"Okay, thanks a lot—bye." I couldn't wait to get out of there.

He watched me as I opened the front door and left. I could tell he was beaming about the whole thing. He even looked better than he usually did. He was happy.

Two weeks later the same scenario unfolded, but I had a feeling the circumstances would not be the same.

My father was busy writing again at the dining room table. He looked up and saw me all dressed up, walking past him on my way to the door.

"Are you going out?"

"Yes, I'm leaving."

"Is she a Greek girl?"

"Actually, no, she's not."

He put his head down and continued writing. Oh, so subtle.

It's amazing to me how one little gesture can say more than a hundred words. But I must say that he never really pushed me or bothered me about associating mainly with Greeks. When John had a huge house party one Saturday evening, it was so crowded you could hardly move from one room to the other.

I was dating a German-Scottish girl at the time named Christine, and I brought her with me to the party. I introduced her to my father, and he was very cordial. He never talked to me about her afterward, either. His way of encouraging me to stay with a Greek girl was to tell stories of Greek men who did not marry Greek girls, but whose lives were unfulfilled because of it. At least that's the way he would always interpret it.

Over one summer I met a girl in Michigan named Martha and would see her every time I went up there, usually during warm days in the summer and autumn. In the meantime, we wrote letters, which would go back and forth every two weeks or so all winter long. Everyone took turns every day to pick up mail from downstairs after George, the mailman, finished his delivery.

Well, my father noticed that these letters, postmarked Benton Harbor, Michigan, were addressed to me and were arriving on a continuous basis. It wasn't long before he brought it to my attention.

"I see you're writing letters to a girl in Benton Harbor?" You couldn't fool him.

"Well, yeah, I guess so." I stumbled for an explanation but couldn't come up with one.

"I know she's not Greek, living in Benton Harbor."

"No," I said. "She's probably Irish."

"Well, it doesn't matter what she is. If I find out you brought her to my house, you'll never go up again."

In this case he didn't differentiate between Greek and any other ethnic group. When any matter involving his home in Michigan was concerned, it was always the same answer—no!

For some reason it seems to be different with daughters than with sons. Most Greek parents, especially fathers, wanted their daughters to marry Greeks. Unfortunately, many times this was caried to extremes.

My sister, Pauline, wanted to marry a man named Paul, who was Polish and Roman Catholic. My parents were vehemently against it and wanted her to stay within her own ethnicity and religion. There was quite a bit of friction among them. Paul is a good man. Pauline made the right decision—she married him. I must say that most people who marry an Orthodox Christian usually convert to Orthodoxy. We must be doing something right.

Even some of my cousins did not marry Greek girls—and they live in Greece! First cousin Lycourgos married Olga, whom he met while going to school in London and who is of Russian background. Costa, another first cousin, married Barbara, who is from Poland. Both are very good women and speak Greek better than most Greek Americans.

One of the things I totally regret in my life has everything to do with Greek girls. It's something I was bitter about for a long time. A friend of mine named Lou approached me from out of the blue.

"Hey Al, Saints Constantine and Helen Church is looking for Greek boys. Did you hear?"

"Did I hear what? Where's St. Constantine anyway? Oh, I remember; it's on Stoney Island Avenue on the South Side. Right?"

"Yeah, that's right."

"What about it?" I was becoming interested.

"They need Greek boys to take part in a ceremony," Lou said.

"Why would I want to be in a ceremony? What kind of ceremony?"

"It's a cotillion, Al."

"What does that involve? I don't know what that is."

"We are going to make a presentation of Greek girls."

"Who are we presenting them to—their third cousins in

Greece?" I tried to be funny, but Lou was dead serious.

"No, no—to society—Greek society," he replied.

"You have got to be joking. Why would I want to be involved in that?"

"They need us—they need us badly. They are having a hard time finding boys to take part in it." Lou was beginning to be persuasive.

"I wonder why? That's the most ridiculous thing I have ever heard of. What did these girls do to make them so special? Did they accomplish anything great that we should applaud them for? Are they honor students? Did they raise money for charity? Did they help support children in an orphanage? The answer is probably none of the above. They are probably there because their parents have money and they want to show off their daughters."

"Yeah, you're probably right, but we have to do it."

"Why do we?"

"Because they have our names and they need us. It's for the Greek community of Chicago. It has to succeed." Lou knew the right answers.

"I don't like it, Lou."

"I know, I don't either. Why don't we do it just one time and no more." He was persistent, but I still wanted to get out of it.

"You said they have our names. Who is *they*?"

"I guess it's the committee that's putting this together. Listen, I'm committed to this thing, but I don't want to go alone. Do it for me, will you?"

"All right. What do I have to do?"

"First, register your name so they know you are on board. Then you'll have to rent a tuxedo."

"A tuxedo? Fancy times, hey?"

"We'll have some fun. It'll be okay."

I must say that the event was presented in an elegant manner with a well-organized presentation of the young ladies, a fine dinner, and quite a bit of both Greek and American dancing. The girls looked quite becoming in their colorful dresses, and the boys looked sharp in their tuxedos. Cameras were clicking all night and rightly so. It was a gala event. I guess I made my contribution to the community. and that's all I can say about it. Would I have done it again? No!

GREEK HERE AND THERE

Most of my life I have heard many references related to being Greek or about Greek culture in general that are foremost in my mind. Some of them are serious and some are amusing. My advisor at Elmhurst College, Dr. Rudolph Schade, was a professor of history and chairman of the history department. I was enrolled in most of his classes, and he was a wonderful instructor. He maintained a distinctive German accent, even though he had been in this country for many years. I could go to his office anytime, and he would always say, "Alex, come in, come in." He was an important inspiration for me.

His classes were always full and included students who weren't even history majors. That's how popular he was on campus. Many years before I was enrolled, he also taught Classical Greek. I still remember when he said in one of his lecture halls, "You cannot be an intellectual, my friends, if you don't know Greek." This statement remained with me for a long time. I was proud.

He amused all the students one day in his Greek history class when he said, "I hate to admit it, but when the Greeks were building magnificent structures throughout the ancient world, creating trigonometry and geometry and attending theatre festivals, my people were swinging from the trees."

In Dr. Schade's History of Rome class, he made a statement that amused all of us. He said, "Let's face it, my friends, a Roman was nothing more than a cheap imitation of a Greek."

Dr. Tarabilda taught international literature at Elmhurst and encouraged his classes to explore world writers and poets. He was a very interesting individual. He included discussions of many modern Greek writers such as Nikos Kazantzakis, Vassilis Vassilikos, and Nobel Laureate poet George Seferis. He made a statement one day which really threw me for a loop. I had never heard this from anybody before. He said, "When I read Nikos Kazantzakis' book *Freedom or Death,* I wished that I had been born Greek."

Initially, I thought he was joking or merely stated the first thing that came to his mind, but when I remembered him clenching his fist when he uttered those words, I realized that this guy meant what he said. The voice of freedom from Turkish oppression resonated through him.

Two men, one Greek and one American, were discussing the attempted Italian invasion of Greece. The Greek explained how the Italians were pushed back into the mountains of Albania after many failed attacks. The Italians could not penetrate the defenders' lines. Commenting on the failure of the Italian Army, the American told the Greek, "I just don't understand it. What does it take to knock off a bunch of restaurants?"

In the popular film *The Robe,* Richard Burton, who played a Roman patrician from a wealthy and influential family, turns to Victor Mature, who played a Greek slave from Corinth, and says, "I am well aware that you Greeks think of us Romans as nothing more than barbarians."

In *Demetrius and the Gladiators,* a sequel to *The Robe,* Victor Mature played Demetrius, who became a hero as a gladiator in the arena. Everyone was talking about "the Greek" and how popular he had become. The emperor Caligula grew tired of hearing about him and, in his frustration, shouted out loud, "The Greek, the Greek—who cares about the Greek?" In extenuating his anger, he cried out as loud as he could for all his court to hear, "Do you know that they cheer him in the streets more than me?" His pride was hurt.

In a Hollywood movie of which the name escapes me, a Greek seaman goes before a court in ancient Rome and explains to the judge why he was nowhere near the scene of a crime that occurred. Apparently, the judge didn't believe his comments and said, "Certainly a Greek could come up with a better story than that."

About twenty years ago, I was taking a survey in Berwyn's Historic Depot District to see how many business owners were interested in having more trees planted in the surrounding area. I came across a man who owned several storefronts with apartments above. We engaged in a conversation about the town, and he told me he bought the property fifteen years before.

He was an Italian American, and he liked the idea of extending the landscaping in the district. As I was taking down his name for approval, he said, "By the way, are you also Italian? You look Italian." I said, "No I'm not. I'm actually Greek." He looked at me and shook his hand up and down and said, "Marone!" I found his reaction amusing, and I took it as a compliment.

George Stoes was building an addition to his home in Michigan, but I can't remember if it was a new room or perhaps an outdoor deck. I asked his wife, Ada, if George did any of the work on the new project himself. Ada replied, "Are you kidding? The only thing Greek men know how to do is make money."

I was conducting an investigation of a company on Chicago's South Side and went to a local diner at lunchtime. Two Chicago police officers came in and sat in a booth directly across from mine. One officer ordered a hamburger with fries, and the other ordered a Greek salad. As the waitress headed toward the kitchen to place the order, the officer who ordered the salad signaled for her to come back to the booth. He asked her, "Can you tell the chef to put extra 'fetus' cheese on the salad?" She looked at him and said, "Certainly, sir."

At Elmhurst College it was generally a rule, although loosely based, that if a professor did not show up for the first ten minutes of a class, it was assumed that he or she wasn't coming and the students could leave. My Classical Greek classroom was located on the third floor of the chapel building on the western edge of the quadrangle. We all sat and waited for professor James Williams to arrive. It was a Friday morning, and we were all anticipating the weekend ahead. Three minutes passed and he hadn't arrived.

Five minutes passed and all eyes and attention were fixated on the classroom clock next to the door. Could it be possible he wasn't going to make it? Our emotions and our hopes were rising by the second. Seven minutes passed, and students were already packing up their notebooks. Some even started putting on their coats and turning sideways in their desks as if they were ready to stand up and leave. The tension was mounting. We were cautiously ecstatic. We were almost home free.

At the eight-minute mark we heard footsteps on the second floor. Could they be those of Professor Williams? God help us! A minute later he walked in, and everyone straightened themselves out in their desks. The suspense was over.

He looked at the clock and said, with a smile on his face, "You don't have to tell me because I know. You had eight minutes of sheer joy!" We all laughed. The ice was broken. We knew he was just as human as the rest of us.

In a history class I taught in Chicago in the 1970s, we were talking about all the aspects of the Trojan War: the reasons behind it, the siege, the Greek and Trojan characters of Achilles, King Menelaus, Hector, and, of course, the Trojan horse. One of my students, Ronald, confronted me in front of the class about the Trojan horse and couldn't wait to give his interpretation of that event: "Mr. Rassogianis, you have to admit it. Your people cheated on that one. You can't get away with it. Let's face it." He said it one more time with emphasis: "Let's face it. You cheated." I must admit that Ronald had a point.

IN RETROSPECT

I almost feel sometimes that I am living in two different worlds, and depending on where I am, I am assuming two different identities. I know that my nationality is American and my ethnicity is Greek, and neither can be changed unless I move to another country, which I do not plan on doing. I guess I can draw on the positive aspects of both, and that has helped me become a little more worldly, if I can use that word.

Many Greek Americans have said that when they are home in the U.S., they are considered to be Greek, and when they are in Greece, they are looked at as Americans. I suppose there is some truth to that. Even Milwaukee Bucks basketball star Giannis Antetokounmpo asked the question, "Who am I? In Greece I was Nigerian, and in Nigeria I was Greek. I was stuck in the middle, living between cultures."

Many have said that we are American only and that the countries of our parents and grandparents fade away with each generation. If my mother and father left Greece and moved to China instead of coming to Chicago, and I grew up in Shanghai, what would I be? Would I be Chinese? Would I look like all the others in my city? I think not. So, what would that make me? I would be what my parents are—Greek, but also a Chinese citizen.

Carl Schurz was a German-born U.S. Senator from Missouri, and a general in the Union Army during the Civil

War. I have always enjoyed this quotation:

I have always been in favor of a healthy Americanization, but that does not mean a complete disavowal of my German heritage. It means that our character should take on the best of that which is American, and combine it with the best of that which is German. By doing so, we can best serve the American people and their civilization.

A group of U.S. senators told a foreign-born member of their body that he should denounce his heritage and the country from which he came and only call himself an American. I believe the senator was also Carl Schurz. To answer their question, he told them that he thought of the United States as his wife and, as such, he would love her, respect her, and be loyal to her. But he also thought of Germany as his mother, whom he also loved. He asked the gentlemen if any of them would take it upon themselves and find it in their hearts to denounce and disregard their own mothers? They looked at each other and bowed their heads. They had nothing to say.

What really puzzles me are Greek American adults who don't know any Greek at all and have no interest in learning it. Some tell me they do not have the time. They are busy round the clock. My response to them is why can't they learn one word per week? How difficult could that be? Others say it isn't really necessary or important to do so. I ask them if it's not important, then why do schools in Germany, France, Britain, and other countries require it in their schools? They know that it's the foundation for Western languages and civilization. Thousands of English words have Greek roots as we all know.

When discussing our church, there are those who want to eliminate the word "Greek" from the Greek Orthodox Church. I have often thought that doing this would be equivalent to organizing a family reunion and inviting every one of your relatives except your mother.

I can't forget that on my many trips to Greece, I have overheard French and Italian tourists speak better Greek than many Greek Americans I know. I'm not just referring to ordering food in a restaurant or asking for directions from the locals, but engaging in conversations. When I listen to them, I can tell they are proud of their ability. It shows.

I have to admit that when I was young, I didn't have much of an interest in anything Greek. I didn't know any better. I wasn't against it, but it didn't interest me very much. Greek school was a chore that I had to tolerate. It wasn't until after my first trip to Greece as a junior in college that I started appreciating the history and culture. I must say I was crazy about both. My advisor and history professor at Elmhurst College, Dr. Rudolph Schade, also had an influence on me.

I find it puzzling whenever I ask someone what their background is and their response is they don't really know. Some say they are not sure. There is such a mixture of nationalities and races in this country, and it's understandable. I am so happy that I have two cultures to draw on, and this has enriched my whole life. Does that make me an admirer of Carl Schurz? I guess it does.

ABOUT THE AUTHOR

Alexander Rassogianis was born in Chicago, Illinois, to parents who emigrated from Sparta, Laconia, Greece. He received a bachelor's degree in history and political science from Elmhurst College and taught history in Chicago for more than fifteen years. He served as a compliance officer and investigated labor discrimination cases for the US government for twenty years. Alex studied international relations in Helsinki, Finland and received a master's degree in history from the University of Wisconsin—Milwaukee in 1982. *Growing Up Greek in Chicago* is his sixth book. He is writing a book of short stories, *Pathways*.

CPSIA information can be obtained
at www.ICGtesting.com
Printed in the USA
JSHW022212020323
38432JS00002B/126